·Believers All·

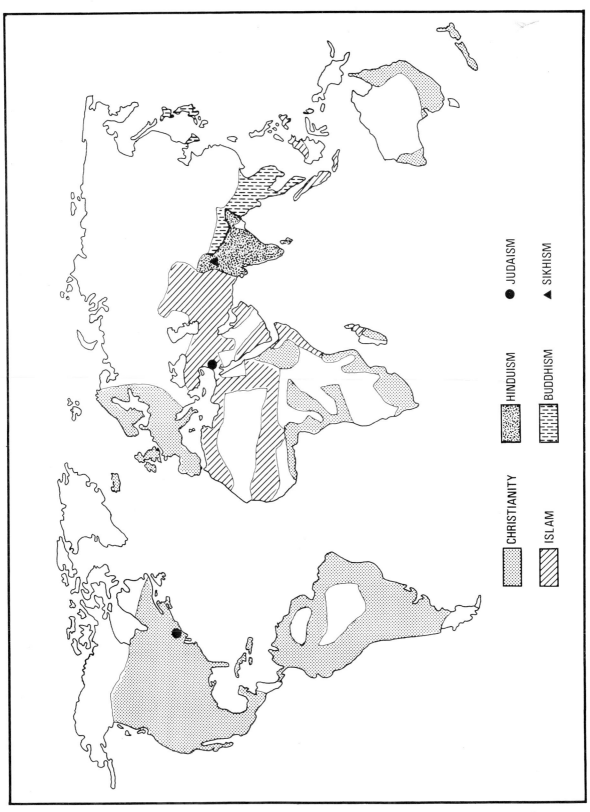

The worldwide distribution of the six religions discussed in this book

CHRISTIANITY

ISLAM

HINDUISM

BUDDHISM

● JUDAISM

▲ SIKHISM

DAVID SIMMONDS

·Believers All·

A BOOK OF
SIX WORLD RELIGIONS

BLACKIE

ISBN 0 216 91574 0

Blackie & Son Ltd
Bishopbriggs, Glasgow G64 2NZ
Furnival House, 14–18 High Holborn, London WC1V 6BX

Printed in Great Britain by Thomson Litho Ltd,
East Kilbride, Scotland

·Contents·

CHAPTER 4   *·Hinduism·*   75

CHAPTER 5   *·Buddhism·*   96

CHAPTER 6   *·Sikhism·*   115

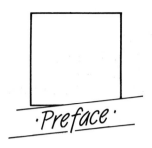

·Preface·

For a considerable time I have been teaching World Religions to examination groups of a wide range of ability. I decided to introduce such a World Religions course for examination at the end of the fifth year, since I consider that an essential part of Religious Education is for young people to study the religious standpoint of ethnic groups which may well form part of their local community. Furthermore, because of the wide coverage of current affairs in the media, young people are bound to be confronted with the problems which arise as a result of the settlement of people from other cultures in their own country. Many communities have to come to terms with these issues and problems, many of which have an important religious element. It is therefore important to include the study of all the major World Religions in the Religious Education of young people in order to help them consider in a serious and constructive way all the relevant issues, and thereby gain as broad an education as possible.

Having made the decision to introduce a World Religions syllabus, I enthusiastically set about preparing to teach the course. It was soon apparent that the available textbooks were not as useful as they seemed at first sight. The result was that over some time I produced a large number of information sheets which I considered contained all that was necessary for sound preparation for the examination. At times a new textbook would appear, but all too often I felt it was lacking in some important aspect. Eventually I decided the only thing to do was to write a textbook myself. For better or for worse, this is the result!

The book is divided into six chapters, each of which concentrates on one particular religion. The religions covered are, first of all, those which have their roots in the Middle East, i.e. Judaism, Christianity and Islam, and then those which developed in the Indian sub-continent, i.e. Hinduism, Buddhism and Sikhism. The book sets out to introduce young people to the beliefs, the worship and the religious practices of the followers of the six faiths. There is an introductory section to each, outlining the origin of the religion and containing, where relevant, a short biography of the founders of the faith. The final part of each describes some of the festivals which followers enjoy celebrating. In order to help students familiarize themselves with the special words and terms of a faith I have included a glossary at the end of each chapter.

I have found this method of presenting the information systematically by topics to be most successful. In my experience, young people cope better with the issues that arise when studying religion once they have a firm grasp of the factual material.

The suggestions for activities at the end of each chapter are designed to make young people think constructively about the various religions so that they can achieve some understanding of other people's religious views and beliefs. The hope is that this will lead to acceptance and toleration of, and perhaps even empathy with, people who live their lives in a very different way.

Finally I must acknowledge the help given to me by my wife and daughter both in reading scripts and making suggestions. Without their assistance I am sure the final version of the book would have been the poorer.

D.S.

·Acknowledgments·

Cover photograph
Network, © Mike Abrahams

Maps
Margaret Dunn

Illustrations
Elizabeth McKay

Photographs
BBC Hulton Picture Library, pages 2, 29, 35 (bottom), 58, 76, 85 (top), 96, 100 (top and bottom)
The United Society for the Propagation of the Gospel, page 4
Council for the Care of Churches, pages 5 (left), 8, 12
British Weekly, page 5 (right)
Barnabys Picture Library, pages 6, 22, 32, 33 (bottom), 40, 42, 44, 47, 80, 88, 89, 101, 102, 103, 124, 125 (bottom)
A Moyes, page 9
Keith Ellis, page 11, supplied by *British Weekly*
The British and Foreign Bible Society, page 16 (left and right)
Carlos Reyes, page 17, supplied by *The Universe*
Raymond Nicholls, page 18, supplied by *The Universe*
The Universe, page 20
Clive Lawton, Board of Deputies of British Jews, pages 30 (top and bottom), 31, 33 (top), 35 (top), 36, 38
Jewish Education Bureau, page 48
Mansell Collection, page 55 (top and bottom)
Douglas Dickins Photo Library, pages 57, 61, 82, 86, 109, 122, 131
Popperfoto, pages 59 (left), 65 (bottom), 79, 97, 99 (right), 111, 117, 130
The Islamic Foundation, pages 59 (right), 64, 69
Philip Emmett, pages 65 (top), 83, 90, 92, 118
Christine Osborne, pages 70, 71
Sally and Richard Greenhill, pages 81, 125 (top), 127 (top and bottom)
Roger Bradley, page 85 (bottom), 116
Dr Dermot Killingley, page 87
Royal Thai Embassy, page 99 (left)
The British Library, page 107

CHAPTER 1

·Christianity·

1 The Life and Teaching of Jesus Christ

Introduction

Christianity derives its name from the founder of the religion, Jesus Christ. (Jesus means 'Saviour', and Christ is from the Greek word *Christos*, 'the Anointed One' or 'Chosen One of God'.) Christians believe that almost 2000 years ago God sent His Son, Jesus, into the world to live a human life. For thirty-three years he lived and worked in Palestine which was then part of the Roman Empire. For only three years he travelled around the country as a wandering preacher, teaching the people to live in God's Way. At first those who believed in Jesus were called 'Followers of the Way'; it was only later that they were called Christians.

The Life of Jesus

Jesus' life was considered such an important event that within 500 years of his birth the Church leaders decided to work out a calendar according to the main events of his life. Thus the years before his birth were called BC, i.e. before Christ, and those following his birth AD, i.e. *Anno Domini*, which is Latin and means 'In the year of our Lord'. However Dionysius, the Christian monk who worked out the dates, made a mistake of about five years when fixing Jesus' birth. Therefore nowadays it is more correct to say that Jesus was born in about 5 BC.

Jesus was a Jew and, except for a brief interval, he lived all his life in Palestine His parents were Joseph and Mary, and they

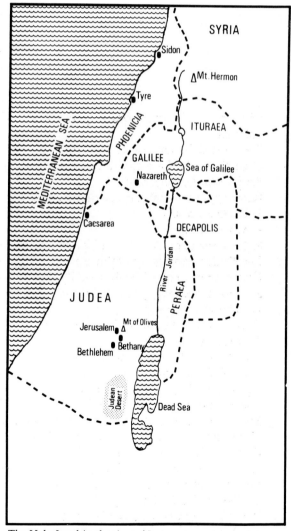

The Holy Land in the time of Jesus

1

learned from God that Mary would bear a son who would be the Messiah and Saviour of the Jews. Messiah was the Hebrew word for 'the Anointed One'. During the reign of Herod the Great in 5 BC Mary and Joseph left their home town of Nazareth and went to Bethlehem in order to take part in a Roman census by registering their names. It was while they were there that Jesus was born. There are various versions but according to the Gospel of Luke in the New Testament the birth took place in a stable because there were no rooms available for Mary and Joseph in any of the inns, and within a short time some shepherds visited the newly-born child.

A 17th-century painting of the Nativity

Soon afterwards the life of the child was threatened by King Herod after Jesus had been visited by three wise men. They came to pay homage to Jesus whom they believed would one day be a king. Joseph took Mary and Jesus to Egypt for safety. After two years they returned to Palestine and settled down in Nazareth where they lived a normal family life. Except for a short visit to the Temple in Jerusalem at the age of twelve, nothing is known about Jesus' life for over thirty years.

At that time the Jews were hoping for the coming of the long-awaited Messiah whom they believed would free them from the foreign rule of the Romans and set up God's Kingdom on Earth. In about AD 27 John the Baptist began preaching. He declared that the Messiah was coming soon and the people should repent. Thousands of Jews responded and were baptized by him in the River Jordan. Jesus then left his settled life in Nazareth and made his way to Judea where he also was baptized by John. Jesus now believed that it was time to begin the work God had given him to do, but he first went into the Judean desert to think about how to carry out this mission. (It was there, the Gospels say, that he was tempted by the devil.) He then returned to Galilee in Northern Palestine and began his work of preaching the coming of God's Kingdom on earth and performing miracles of healing. He chose twelve close companions (the Twelve Disciples), and for the next two to three years worked in Galilee, but occasionally also visited Jerusalem.

At Passovertime (see page 51) in AD 29 Jesus went to Jerusalem with his disciples. This was a direct challenge to the Jewish religious leaders who were increasingly hostile to his work. This hostility became very strong after the people of Jerusalem had welcomed him as he rode into the city on an ass, and after he had driven the traders and moneychangers out of the courtyard of the Temple, as he believed they were defiling God's House. A few days later Jesus and his disciples met quietly together in a house in Jerusalem for what Christians now call the Last Supper. That night he was arrested by Temple Guards, who were guided by Judas Iscariot, a disciple who betrayed him. This happened on the slopes of the Mount of Olives, as Jesus and his disciples were returning to the village of Bethany where they were staying. Within twenty-four hours he had been tried by both the Jewish and Roman authorities, and executed by crucifixion. Shortly after he died, his body was buried in a rock tomb.

Within three days his disciples and other

followers were utterly convinced that he had risen from the dead as he said he would. Over the next few weeks he appeared to them on many occasions and taught them more of the Gospel. Finally he met them on the Mount of Olives and after giving them instructions to preach the Gospel 'to the ends of the Earth', he left them and ascended to heaven. A few days later at the Feast of Pentecost the disciples and their friends were filled with the Holy Spirit, as Jesus had promised, and from that time on they boldly preached the message of the Gospel. From these very small beginnings Christianity spread to become numerically the largest religion in the world. Today there are Christians in every continent, and in nearly every country.

Christianity may be regarded as one religion but in fact the Christian Church has many branches, each with variations in their beliefs, form of worship, celebration of festivals, etc. The various branches or denominations, as they are called, can be grouped roughly into three:

Orthodox, e.g. Greek Orthodox
Roman Catholic
Reformed (sometimes called Protestant), e.g. Church of England, Church of Scotland, Methodist, Baptist, etc.

Even within these groups there is a wide range of practices and we cannot cover them all in a book of this size. But, despite the variations, all the Churches base their beliefs about the right and wrong way of living on the teaching of Jesus and that is what unites them.

The Teaching of Jesus

From the very beginning of his ministry Jesus set out to teach people about the Kingdom of God, by which he meant the rule of God in their lives. He called God 'Father' and by this he meant that God looks after people in an even more caring way than the kindest human father. Jesus showed how God cares by mixing with the outcasts and the downtrodden and unfortunate people in life. He never failed to help anyone who came to him in real need. His greatest act of love was to die willingly.

Jesus taught people not to worry about anything in life. He said if they allowed God to control their lives they would find it much easier to face any difficulties. He knew this was not easy, especially as there was so much evil in the world against which his followers must continually fight. He said that people cannot avoid suffering, but those who followed him would be able to cope with it, and even use it to advantage. Jesus also told his followers that everyone must face judgment when those who have sinned will be punished, and the faithful will be rewarded. This will be when evil is finally overthrown and God's reign is universal.

Although Jesus never really said who he was, he called himself 'Son of Man'—this probably means that he considered he was chosen by God to be the Leader of his Kingdom. In the end his disciples came to believe that he was the Messiah. In his teaching he made several claims, e.g.

that he had the power to forgive sins,
that by his death men would be saved from sin and so be brought back to God,
that he would live again after his death,
at the end of time he would return to judge all people.

Throughout his teaching ministry Jesus preached his message to anyone who would listen. He hoped that his own people would accept it first, but when they rejected it he told his disciples to take it to the whole world. By what he said, Jesus taught people that they were most important to God, and that they should accept God as Father. He himself set the example by his own life of faith and prayer. In order to enter into this special relationship with God, Jesus said that people must repent, i.e. feel the need of God's forgiveness, and then trust God absolutely. Then the rule of God can begin in people's lives, and it will be seen by the way God guides them, through the response He makes to their prayers. However Jesus gave a stern warning: that those who rejected his teaching would, in effect, judge themselves. They would condemn themselves by allowing sin to become a stronger force in their lives. This is why Jesus strongly condemned those who led selfish and useless lives.

Jesus gave the clearest outline of his teaching in the Sermon on the Mount. In this sermon are found many examples of how his followers should live. For instance, people should have great respect for family life and marriage, they should generously help those in need, and even respect their enemies. He said the guiding rule for people's behaviour should be 'treat others as you want them to treat you'. Finally Jesus said that there were really only two commandments for people to keep: Love God and Love your fellow men. This is not just teaching about good behaviour. It is deeply religious teaching about trust in God, and about being prepared to forgive people because God forgives them.

Christianity in practice today—this baby clinic in Ummedpur is run by the Church of North India

2 Christian Initiation and Other Ceremonies

The Christian faith has initiation ceremonies by which a person becomes a member of the Church. In general there are two separate ceremonies. The first is baptism, performed in infancy, and the second, confirmation, which is held in adolescence.

Baptism
The customary time for this ceremony is when a baby is two or three months old. The ceremony is a service held in church around the font. The font is a special basin on a stand containing the water to be used at the baptism. It is often placed near the main door of a church as a symbol of entering into the membership of God's family. However in some churches it is placed at the front near the pulpit or preaching desk.

The baptism ceremony is conducted by a priest, vicar or minister. For convenience we will use the one term—priest. Besides the baby, the parents and godparents, there may also be present other relations, friends and members of the congregation. The service may begin with a baptismal hymn, after which prayers are said. A suitable passage from one of the Gospels in the New Testament is then read aloud. Next the priest blesses the baby and the parents, and in some churches the godparents make special promises on the child's behalf. They promise to teach the child to fight against evil, to instruct the child in the teaching of Jesus Christ, and to bring up the child in the family of the Church, so giving it a firm Christian training. The priest then takes the baby in his arms and names it saying, 'I baptize you in the name of the Father, and the Son and the Holy Spirit. Amen.' He puts water on the baby's head, making the sign of the cross, and gives it the kiss of peace. He then returns the baby to its mother. The service ends with a blessing spoken by the priest.

At the end of the service, baptism by total immersion in a special baptismal tank is carried out by the minister of the church. In the Baptist Church this ceremony is in place of the confirmation rite which is conducted in other churches.

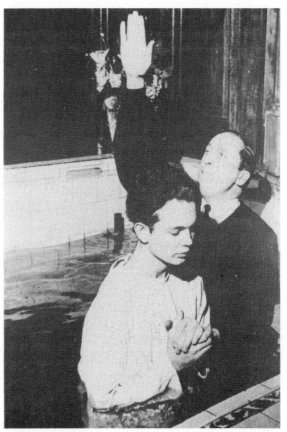

An adult baptism

An infant baptism

In the Baptist Church there is no baptism of infants since Baptists believe that they are too young to understand the promises that are being made. Instead a short service of thanksgiving to God is performed in church during which the baby is given its name. Baptism takes place when a person is of an age to understand fully the meaning of the Christian faith, and is ready to accept all the responsibilities and duties of Church membership. A special service is held in church during which the person being baptized makes a public declaration of faith in Christ.

Confirmation

The ceremony takes place when a child has grown up and is responsible for his own actions; this is usually in late adolescence but in the Roman Catholic Church it is usually at an earlier age. After the course of study led by the priest of the church, when all aspects of the Christian faith are considered, a special service takes place in church.

In front of the whole congregation the young person confirms his or her wish to follow Christ and accept all the responsibilities and duties of living a Christian life.

(In fact the promises made at baptism are confirmed.) In many churches, particularly the Church of England and the Roman Catholic Church, a bishop conducts the most important part of the service. He asks these three important questions:

'Do you turn to Christ?

Are you sorry for your sins?

Do you turn away from sin?'

After the young person has answered 'Yes' to each question, the bishop puts his hands on the person's head and says 'Confirm, O Lord, your servant with your Holy Spirit'. This action is called the 'laying-on of hands', and it is believed God's Holy Spirit passes into the person at that moment. The service then concludes with the celebration of Holy Communion with the newly-confirmed people receiving communion first.

In some churches, as there are no bishops, the minister conducts the whole service. In the Methodist Church, besides the 'laying-on of hands' by the minister, the Senior Church Steward, on behalf of the congregation, shakes each person by the hand, welcoming them into full membership of the Church. Thus the young people are accepted into the family of the Church. They begin a new life, one of personal devotion to God and to the Church.

Marriage

In many Christian countries it is not necessary to be married in church since, in the eyes of the law, marriage is a legal contract made between two people. The ceremony can therefore be held in a registry office and be conducted by the local registrar. On the other hand, a wedding in church has an important religious meaning. It is a union of a man and a woman on which God's blessing is given. In the Church of England before the wedding takes place the Banns must be read out in church on three successive weeks. These state that anyone wishing to object to a wedding taking place should say so before the ceremony is held.

The form of a wedding service is much the same in all churches. Before the bride arrives, the bridegroom and his best man sit at the front of the church. The best man is his attendant, often a brother or close friend. All the relatives and friends sit in the seats behind them. The bride, often veiled and wearing a white dress, is brought into the church by her father or a male relative, attended by the bridesmaid(s). They then stand next to the groom and his best man.

The priest begins the service by saying that all are present in the sight of God to witness the joining in holy matrimony of the bride and groom. The couple make important promises to each other. The groom says that he will 'love, comfort, and honour his wife, and keep her in sickness and health, and forsake all others'. The bride, in turn, promises to do the same for her husband—she may also make a promise to obey him. The priest asks the bride's father if he agrees to 'giving away' his daughter to the groom. After this the best man gives the wedding ring to the priest who blesses it, and the groom then places it on the third finger of the bride's left hand as he says 'with this ring I thee wed'. The bride may also give a ring to the groom in a similar way.

The priest next conducts prayers during which everyone present expresses the hope that the newly-married couple will keep the

A Christian marriage ceremony

promises they have made, and that 'they may ever remain in perfect love and peace together'. Often the priest gives a short address usually directed to the bride and groom about the duties and responsibilities of married life. The ceremony ends with the words, 'These whom God hath joined together, let no man put asunder', and a final hymn is sung, followed by the Benediction. In some churches the bride and groom also take Holy Communion—this is usually the case in the Roman Catholic Church.

The bride and groom and their parents and witnesses then go and sign the register and the marriage certificate in the church vestry. They are now legally married. As they leave the church they may be showered with confetti and rice. These are symbols of fertility and this is how everyone wishes they will have many children! Photographs of the wedding party are taken. The bridal party and their guests go to the wedding reception and afterwards the newly-married couple leave for their honeymoon.

A Funeral Service
When a Christian dies the family mourns the loss of a loved one. The service is always a solemn occasion, but it is not gloomy, since Christians believe that death is not the end of life. They believe that Christians live on eternally in peace with God after their life on earth ends. So hope is the theme of a Christian funeral service.

After the person's body has been prepared and put into a coffin, a simple ceremony might take place in church in the presence of the dead person's relatives and friends. The coffin is carried into the church and placed at the front. Appropriate hymns, prayers and passages of scripture are included in the service. The priest usually gives an address during which he thanks God for the life of the dead person and offers words of comfort to the relatives.

The coffin is then taken either to be buried in a cemetery or for cremation at a crematorium. The priest offers more prayers as the coffin is lowered into the grave and covered with earth (or as it disappears from sight at the crematorium). If no service is held at the church, then the only service would be at the cemetery or crematorium. Then the relatives and friends return to the home of the bereaved or a hotel for a meal together. People usually express their sympathy by sending messages of comfort, gifts of flowers, or by contributing money which the family donates to a particular charity.

3 The Christian Place of Worship

The building where Christians meet to worship God is called a church. This word comes from the Greek language and it means 'the Lord's House'. There are many types of church but the most common in Britain are either parish churches, which could be Church of England (or Scotland, Wales or Ireland) or Roman Catholic, or Free Churches (mainly Methodist, Baptist or United Reform). All these churches have many features in common, but there are a number of important differences.

Parish Churches
The plan of most parish churches is in the form of a cross, although in more recent years churches have been built with rectangular and even circular plans. The cross symbolizes the death and resurrection of Jesus Christ. Churches are built so that the altar, the most prominent feature, is at the eastern end, i.e. so that worshippers face towards the rising sun. Churches have been built facing this particular direction since the late 4th century AD (see plan of parish church). The churches are usually built of stone, and at the opposite end from the altar there is a tower which contains the belfry where the church bells are hung. These are rung to call the people to church for worship, and whenever special services are being held, such as

A typical country parish church

weddings and funerals. Some churches have a tall spire built on, or instead of, the tower. The spire points upwards to remind people of heaven.

The main door of a parish church is at the western end, often under a porch. Just inside the door stands the font, where baptism services are held. The main part of the church is the nave, which contains the pews (seats) where the congregation sits. The church has two side bays, one to the north and the other to the south. In these are small side chapels, one of which will be the Lady Chapel dedicated to the Virgin Mary. The remainder of the church is called the chancel, and it is separated from the nave by an open screen. In some churches on the top of this screen there is a crucifix with figures of St John and the Virgin Mary on either side. This is called the rood screen; rood is an old word for crucifix. In front of the screen at one side is the pulpit which is used by the priest for preaching, and on the other side is a lectern or stand on which is placed the Holy Bible used during the services for readings.

The chancel has two sections, the first being the choir where the clergy (priests) and the choir sit. It also contains the organ which is used to accompany the singing of the choir and congregation. At the far end of the chancel, separated from the choir by a rail, is the sanctuary in which the altar or holy table is situated. The altar is a type of table made from wood or stone, which is used during the service of Holy Communion. The altar is usually covered with a special cloth, and has a cross and candles standing on it.

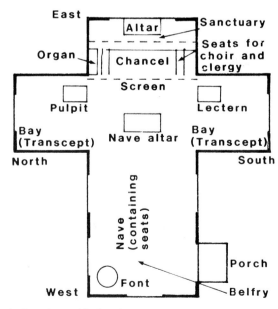

A plan of a parish church

Somewhere in the sanctuary a small lamp may be kept burning. This is to show that in a small cupboard nearby the reserved sacrament is kept. This sacrament is bread and wine which is used when the priest visits members of the church who cannot attend the celebration of Holy Communion in church. Many ancient parish churches also contain tombs and statues commemorating important people who lived in the parish. Many of the windows are of stained glass showing scenes from the Bible or pictures of the saints.

Roman Catholic churches contain other features which they consider to be important. There are confession boxes where, in complete privacy, people confess their sins to the priest and ask for forgiveness. Often on the altar there is a small box or cupboard called the tabernacle which contains the reserved sacrament. Around the walls of the church is a series of pictures or carved reliefs called the Stations of the Cross. These show the last journey of Jesus when he carried his cross to the place of His Crucifixion. The Lady Chapel is more elaborate as it always contains a statue of the Virgin Mary, and many lighted candles which have been placed there by people when they have offered prayers of petition to God. At each entrance to the church there is a small basin called a stoop containing a little water. As they enter the church the people dip their fingers in the water and make the sign of the cross on their foreheads.

The Free Churches

The Free Churches usually have the same features as a parish church, but they may be placed in a different position, and often the church has a rectangular plan. The sanctuary at the front of the church contains in the centre a very large pulpit on which there is a stand for the Bible. The communion table (or altar) stands in front of the pulpit with the font to one side. A communion rail separates the sanctuary from the rest of the church. The organ is usually positioned behind the pulpit with the choir seats ranged along each side. In large Free Churches a gallery runs

A room used for confession in a Roman Catholic church

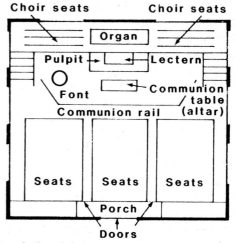

A plan of a free church

round three sides of the building. The reason for this arrangement is that the preaching of God's Word is generally considered the most important part of worship, so the pulpit must occupy a prominent place at the front of the church.

Cathedrals

A cathedral is a very large church. It has the same basic shape and same features as a parish church, but it is much more elaborate. The Church of England and the Roman Catholic Church divide the country up into areas called dioceses. A bishop is in charge of a diocese and the cathedral is its main church (it is sometimes called the Mother Church of the diocese). The cathedral contains the bishop's throne called the *cathedra*, and this is where the name 'cathedral' originates.

4 Christian Worship

Introduction

The holy day of the Christians is Sunday, the first day of the week. It was on the first day of the Jewish week that Jesus rose from the dead. Thus whenever Christians meet for worship on a Sunday they are reminded of their basic belief in Jesus' resurrection. It is also called 'the Lord's Day' and is the equivalent of the Jewish Sabbath or day of rest.

Forms of Worship

The Christian Churches have various distinctive ways of worshipping God, but in all forms of worship there are common elements such as singing hymns and psalms, reading from the Bible, saying prayers and preaching sermons. Different churches emphasize different ways of worship, for instance, the celebration of Mass in the Roman Catholic Church and the preaching of God's Word in the Free Churches. Most churches have a set pattern for their services or forms of worship which are written out in special service books. For Roman Catholics the book is the Missal, for members of the Church of England the Book of Common Prayer or the New Alternative Service Book, and for Methodists, there is the New Service Book and in the Church of Scotland it is the Book of Common Order.

Mass or Holy Communion

Mass is perhaps the most important Christian service, especially for the Roman Catholic Church. It is a celebration of the last meal ('The Last Supper') Jesus had with his disciples before his crucifixion. It is sometimes called the Eucharist, meaning 'thanksgiving'.

Roman Catholic Mass begins with a hymn, after which everyone says 'In the name of the Father, of the Son and of the Holy Spirit', and then makes the sign of the cross. Next, between the singing of a psalm and a special chant of praise called the Gloria (it begins 'Glory to God on high'), an important prayer asking God for forgiveness is recited. There follows the reading of passages from the Bible, and the people affirm their Christian faith by repeating together the Nicene Creed. The priest offers prayers of supplication to God, and the people recite a special prayer to the Virgin Mary which begins 'Hail, Mary, full of grace'. This section of the Mass closes with the singing or reciting of an old Latin hymn called the Sanctus: it begins with the words 'Holy, Holy, Holy Lord'.

The priest then consecrates the bread and wine. The passage from the New Testament is read which explains how Jesus instructed his followers to remember what he had done for them when at the Last Supper he broke the bread and blessed the wine. More prayers are said, concluding with everyone saying the Lord's Prayer. Then comes the Peace: the priest offers the Peace of the Lord to the people by placing his hands together and bowing slightly towards them. The people respond by making the sign of the

Peace to each other, or by shaking hands with their neighbours.

The breaking of bread now takes place. (The bread is in the form of a wafer.) The priest breaks off a small piece of wafer and drops it into a chalice of wine, while the people say an old hymn which asks Jesus to forgive his followers. It begins 'Lamb of God, who takes away the sins of the World, have mercy upon us'. The people then take the communion by going to the altar rail and, while kneeling, receive a small piece of wafer which is held over the chalice of wine while it is given. Once all the people have received communion, the priest drinks the wine. The Mass then ends with the priest offering prayers of dismissal and saying the Benediction.

A priest distributes the elements during a Church of England communion service

In some Roman Catholic churches, at times during the service a small bell is rung to signify that an important part of the service has been reached. Also incense is burned in a special container called a thurible. The sweet-smelling fragrance reminds the people of the presence of God (since fragrance was once considered to be a divine gift) and also acts as an offering to Him.

In the last few years there has been a change in the celebration of Mass. The priest now faces the congregation as he conducts the service. In some churches another altar has been erected immediately in front of the congregation in the nave, and as a result the people feel that they are more involved in the service. Also, in the last twenty years Mass has been celebrated in the native language of each country, not in Latin, which had been used since the very early days of the Church.

Holy Communion in Other Churches

The other main Churches generally follow the same pattern in Holy Communion as the Roman Catholics, but with some important variations. In the Church of England the service of Holy Communion or Parish Communion is becoming the most important service to be held on Sunday morning. At the service the people receive both the bread and wine, and the priest drinks any wine that remains. In the Free Churches the wine is given to the people in small individual glasses, and in some of these churches (mainly the United Reform) the bread and wine is taken to the people as they sit in the pews. At the appropriate time everyone eats the bread together, then drinks the wine. However, in general, the Free Churches do not celebrate Holy Communion as frequently as the other Churches.

Other Services in Church

In the Church of England and in the Free Churches other types of service besides Holy Communion are used. The service which may be used in the morning in the Church of England is called Matins, and the evening service is Evensong. The order of service for Matins is as follows:

The choir and priest enter while the first hymn is sung.

The priest reads passages of scripture which urge the people to confess their sins.

Prayers of Confession are said by the priest.

The Lord's Prayer is spoken together.

The Venite (a special prayer which begins 'O come let us sing unto the Lord') is sung.

A Psalm from the Old Testament is sung together.

The priest reads from the Old Testament.

The people sing the Te Deum (another special psalm; it begins 'We praise thee, O God').

The priest reads from the New Testament.

The people sing a further special psalm called the Benedictus which begins 'Blessed be the Lord God of Israel'.

The Apostles' Creed: every one stands and says together this statement of what they believe; the first words are 'I believe in God the Father Almighty, Maker of Heaven and Earth'.

Prayers are said by the priest for other people.

The sermon is given by the priest.

The Offering is collected, usually during the singing of a hymn.

The Benediction, i.e. a closing prayer is given by the priest.

The service of Evensong is very similar in form to Matins.

A service in progress inside a parish church

In the Free Churches a simple form of service is usually used, as can be seen from the following order:

Hymn: usually in praise of God
Prayers: Confession and Thanksgiving
Hymn
Bible Reading: from the Old Testament
Hymn
Bible Reading: from the New Testament
Prayers of Intercession: that is for others and for themselves
Offering: followed by a short prayer of dedication
Hymn
Sermon: the preacher addresses the congregation, often using a verse from the Bible readings as his subject
Hymn
Benediction: closing prayer

The preacher who is in charge of the service may arrange the order as he chooses. In this type of service the most important parts are the reading of the Bible and the preaching of the sermon which are thought of as 'the Word of God'.

The Practice of Prayer in Christianity

Christians are encouraged to pray to God regularly. There are no compulsory rules concerning daily devotions. However, they believe it is necessary to improve their spiritual lives by communicating with God by praying each day. When praying, Christians often say four different types of prayer. The word ACTS reminds them of these:

A: Adoration: that is praising God.
C: Confession: confessing sin and asking God for forgiveness.
T: Thanksgiving: thanking God for everything in life.
S: Supplication: asking God for help and guidance both for themselves and for others.

The best-known prayer of the Christian faith was given to the twelve disciples when they asked Jesus how they should pray. It is called the Lord's Prayer and contains most of the four elements above.

Many Christians put aside some time each day for private devotions. They will ask God first of all to guide their thoughts, then they will read a short passage from the Bible. They think about the meaning of the passage and work out how to apply its teaching in their lives. Next they spend several minutes praying to God, praising and thanking Him, asking for forgiveness and seeking help for other people and finally for themselves. To complete this time of devotion they may remain silent in the belief that God will speak to them.

When praying, Christians very often kneel down on a low stool or a cushion. (In parish churches these are provided for the people to use.) They bow their heads and close their eyes and perhaps put their hands together. This helps them to concentrate their thoughts on God. Many prayers are written down in the Service Books; they are read either aloud or silently, or learnt by heart. People use religious objects which help them to think of God while praying, e.g. a cross or a crucifix. The most commonly used object is a rosary, which is a string of fifty beads with a small crucifix attached. The beads are counted as the prayers are spoken.

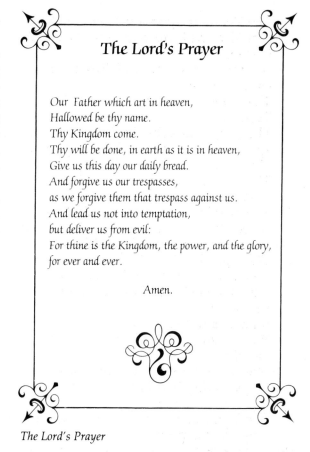

The Lord's Prayer

Our Father which art in heaven,
Hallowed be thy name.
Thy Kingdom come.
Thy will be done, in earth as it is in heaven,
Give us this day our daily bread.
And forgive us our trespasses,
as we forgive them that trespass against us.
And lead us not into temptation,
but deliver us from evil:
For thine is the Kingdom, the power, and the glory,
for ever and ever.

Amen.

The Lord's Prayer

5 Christian Beliefs: The Creed

As in most of the main religions of the world, the beliefs of the Christian faith are summarized in a statement which is called a creed. The word 'creed' comes from the Latin *credo* which means 'I believe'. There are two creeds in Christianity which are regularly used in devotions. The Apostles' Creed first appeared in the 2nd century and it is a summary of what the Apostles or disciples taught. The Nicene Creed was written in the 4th century following the Council of Nicea in AD 325. This council attempted to explain more clearly the Christian belief concerning the nature of Jesus Christ, i.e. how he could be both human and divine at the same time. The Nicene Creed gives a clear statement of the council's conclusions. It must be remembered that the creeds were written in the religious language of their day.

The Apostles' Creed
This creed is really divided up into three sections. The first describes the nature of God. The next and main section concerns the life and work of Jesus Christ, and the third section first refers to the Holy Spirit, and then deals with beliefs concerning the Church and the lives of individual Christians.

The Meaning of the Creed
The first section states clearly that God exists. He is the Supreme Being who has created the Universe and everything in it, including mankind, yet He is a Father who loves His Creation.

The second section shows that Jesus was a

historical figure since he lived in Palestine as a man almost 2000 years ago. In the life of Jesus, God showed what He Himself is like; when people look at Jesus they see God. God's purpose is to bring people back to Him. But this could only be accomplished by Jesus' death on the cross and his raising back to life by God. The creed goes on to say that Jesus is now in heaven where he lives on in the presence of God, and that at some unknown time in the future he will judge all mankind according to their actions and beliefs when they lived on earth.

In the final section the creed first explains that the power of God is at work in the world through the Holy Spirit. Then it shows that the Church is the holy, worldwide body of Christian people, and that individual Christians, as a result of belief in Jesus, can be forgiven their sins. After death, they will live on, in a different form, with God for ever.

Thus Christians say that Jesus was not just a great prophet. He had a very special relationship with God, which the creeds describe as that between a father and a son. Also God allowed Jesus to die so that He could show His love for all people, and renew the covenant that He has made between Himself and the Jewish people in the time of Abraham and Moses. This new covenant is between God and all people, and it is available to all who believe in Jesus. It is clearly expressed in a verse from St John's Gospel in the New Testament which says 'God loved the world so much that He gave His only Son so that everyone who believes in Him may not die but have eternal life.' (John 3:16)

6 The Christian Holy Book

The Holy Bible contains the sacred writings of Christians. Christians call the contents of the book 'the Word of God', since they believe that through it God speaks to His people. Christians also say that the book reveals the truth about God and that it shows them how they should live.

The Bible takes its name from Byblos, the city where the best papyrus was made. The Christians wanted to write their scriptures on the best possible papyrus, hence the chosen name. It is really a collection of books. These books were written in several languages, e.g. Hebrew, Aramaic, Greek, between 900 BC and AD 100 by many varied authors. They contain a wide variety of literature, for instance, legends, poems, hymns, prayers, history, laws, letters and sermons. The Bible is divided into two parts: the Old Testament and the New Testament. The word 'testament' means 'covenant' or 'agreement', and the two parts explain the nature of these covenants and how they influenced the early Christians in their dealings with God and in their daily lives.

The Old Testament
The Old Testament is an account of how God revealed himself to the Jews. He taught them how to live in His Way by giving them His Law. The book also shows how, over the centuries, God's prophets revealed more of His Nature. In the Old Testament there are thirty-nine books of differing types, i.e.

Laws:	Genesis, Exodus, Leviticus, Numbers, Deuteronomy
History:	Joshua, Judges, 1 and 2 Samuel, 1 and 2 Kings, 1 and 2 Chronicles, Ezra, Nehemiah
Stories:	Ruth, Esther, Daniel, Jonah
Poetry:	Job, Psalms, Song of Solomon, Lamentations
Wisdom:	Proverbs, Ecclesiastes
Prophets:	Isaiah, Jeremiah, Ezekiel, Hosea, Joel, Amos, Obadiah, Micah, Nahum, Habakkuk, Zephaniah, Haggai, Zechariah, Malachi

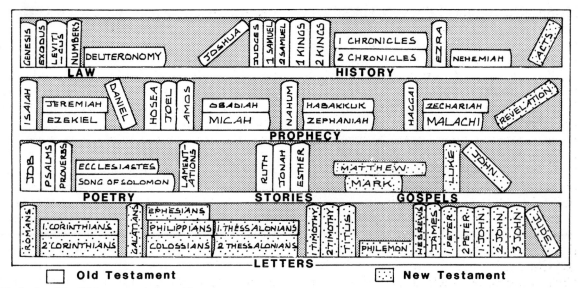

Old Testament | New Testament

The books of the Bible represented as a library

The New Testament

The second part of the Bible describes how God showed himself finally through the life, work and resurrection of Jesus Christ. By this means God taught in a much clearer way how He wants people to live their lives. The first four books of the New Testament are called 'Gospels', which is an old word meaning 'Good News'. The writers of the Gospels describe the life and teaching of Jesus which, they say, is 'Good News'. Other books in this testament outline the growth of the Early Church and the many problems it faced. Much of this information is recorded in letters sent to different churches and to individual Christians. Altogether there are twenty-seven books in the New Testament. They are as follows:

The Gospels:	St Matthew, St Mark, St Luke, St John
History:	the Acts of the Apostles; a description of the Early Church written by St Luke
Letters:	written by St Paul to Churches he had established and to Christian friends: Romans, 1 and 2 Corinthians, Galatians, Ephesians, Philippians, Colossians, 1 and 2 Thessalonians, 1 and 2 Timothy, Titus, Philemon
Letters:	written by other Christians: Hebrews, James, 1 and 2 Peter, 1, 2, and 3 John, Jude
The Revelation of Saint John:	this describes a series of visions in which John imagined evil being overthrown and heaven being established on earth

The Bible in Worship

Since Christians regard the Bible as the textbook of their faith, it is used regularly in both public and private worship. Christians constantly feel the need to be reminded of Bible teaching, and so sections (usually called 'lessons') are read aloud during public worship. Passages relating the life and teaching of Jesus are especially used. Whenever a sermon is preached in church, the preacher nearly always uses a 'text', i.e. a verse or phrase taken from the Bible reading as his theme. In some Free Churches, such as the United Reformed Church, the importance of the Bible is emphasized at the beginning of the service when the book is carried to the pulpit and placed open upon it. Also people frequently use the Bible in their private devotions and in study groups. They read and study particular passages so that they can learn more about living a Christian life.

A Bible reading in a busy shopping centre

The Old Testament was first written in Hebrew and the New Testament partly in Greek and Aramaic. Then a Latin version was produced. It was the middle of the 16th century before attempts at an English translation were made by Tyndale and Coverdale and not until 1611 that the Authorized Version appeared and became recognized as a literary classic. It was at least another 250 years before there was a revival of interest in revisions and translations in Britain and America and by different denominations.

A selection of various modern English translations of the Bible

Notably we have had the English Revised Version, the Moffat Translation, The Revised Standard Version, Phillips Translation, the Jerusalem Bible, The New English Bible, and the Good News Bible, the latter a particularly clear and easy-to-read version in modern English.

7 Pilgrimage in Christianity

Pilgrimage has never been regarded as essential in Christianity. However, throughout the centuries since the beginnings of the faith, Christians have visited places associated with the life of Jesus and with the lives of important Christian saints, and also places where visions, especially of the Virgin Mary, have been seen.

For Christians Israel (formerly called Palestine) is very important because it is where Jesus lived and worked. Many places in the Holy Land associated with him have long been centres of pilgrimage, and are visited by thousands of Christians each year. Jerusalem is particularly important since the events concerning his arrest, crucifixion and resurrection took place there. At the places thought to be connected with these events churches have been built, e.g. at the hill of execution and at the tomb where Jesus was buried. Also every year during Holy Week on Good Friday many pilgrims like to follow the route Jesus took when he carried the cross on which he was crucified. This is known as the Way of the Cross or Via Dolorosa.

Bethlehem is another town in Israel visited by Christian pilgrims. There is a church built over the site of the stable where it is believed Jesus was born. This church is called the Church of the Holy Nativity. In the north of Israel, around the Sea of Galilee, there are many places associated with Jesus visited by pilgrims, for instance, the Mount of Transfiguration (Mount Hermon), the field where he fed the crowd of 5000 people, and the hill where he preached the Sermon on the Mount.

In Europe there are many towns which became famous centres of pilgrimage, especially in the Middle Ages. Santiago de Compostela in Spain has been visited by pilgrims ever since the 9th century because it is traditionally the site of the grave of the Apostle James. Rome is also a place of pilgrimage because of its many associations with the Church. It is said that the great church dedicated to St Peter contains his tomb, and perhaps that of St Paul as well. Today, since the city contains the Vatican Palace, the home of the Pope or head of the Roman Catholic Church, many Roman Catholics like to make a visit there, especially at festival time, when the Pope blesses the crowd assembled in St Peter's Square.

In Britain there are a number of sites that have long been visited by pilgrims. The most famous is the shrine of St Thomas à Becket who was murdered beside the altar in Canterbury Cathedral. Walsingham, in Norfolk, was another famous pilgrimage centre in England. A shrine to the Virgin Mary was built there in the 11th century, and until the time of Henry VIII pilgrims came there from all over France. Henry ordered the shrine to

A national pilgrimage to Walsingham

be destroyed, but in 1921 the pilgrimages were revived. Two modern shrines were built: one for Roman Catholics and the other for Anglicans (members of the Church of England). Nowadays members from both churches visit the shrines regularly. There have been similar revivals of pilgrimage to important Christian centres in the north of England and in Scotland. Annual pilgrimages take place to St Cuthbert's tomb in Durham Cathedral, to Lindisfarne (Holy Island) off the coast of Northumberland which St Aidan made the base of his mission of spreading the Christian message in Northern Britain, and in Scotland to the island of Iona which has long been a Christian stronghold, in fact ever since St Columba landed there from Ireland in AD 597. In Ireland, the tomb of St Patrick is visited at Downpatrick.

Modern Christian pilgrims visit all these places to pray and to seek for spiritual refreshment and guidance. However, there are two places in Western Europe which have become important for people suffering from serious illnesses and physical handicaps of all types. These are Lourdes in France and Knock in Ireland. In both places

The blessing of the sick during a pilgrimage to Lourdes

visions of the Virgin Mary were seen during the last century. At Lourdes a young girl named Bernadette said she saw a vision of the Virgin Mary on eighteen separate occasions. On one of these appearances a spring of water began to flow out of the ground from a spot which the Virgin indicated. Many believe that the water from this spring has miraculous powers. Soon after these visions there were reports of people who visited the places being cured of illness. Since then, particularly at Lourdes, there have been many reported cures amongst the many thousands of sick people who have visited the shrines. Even if the sick are not restored to health they always return home feeling physically, mentally and spiritually renewed.

8 Fasting

In the early days of the Church, fasting was an important duty undertaken by the majority of Christians. However as the centuries passed, its observance became less strict, and it was followed mainly by priests and by those living in closed communities such as monks and nuns.

The period of Lent has always been associated with fasting. Lent is the forty days of the Christian calendar from Ash Wednesday to the day before Easter Sunday. The name 'Lent' comes from an old English word meaning 'Spring', as the fast was always held at that time of the year. Lent reminds

Christians of the time when Jesus spent forty days fasting in the desert during which period he was tempted. For Christians Lent can be a period of fasting, meditation and penance (i.e. asking for forgiveness and making up for wrong-doing). In this way they prepare for the celebrations at Easter. Before celebrating Christ's resurrection, a Christian first remembers the crucifixion. They examine their lives and consider whether they have lived according to Christ's teaching, and they make a firm resolution to improve their Christian living.

In the early days of the Church Lent was a short but very strict fast for adults who were to be baptized as Christians on the Saturday before Easter Day. As time passed the fast was extended to include all the forty days of Lent, but it became less strict and was followed by all Christians. Nowadays Christians take Lent less seriously; there is little or no fasting, but some people give up trivial things, e.g. sweets, smoking, etc. during the season as a reminder of Lent.

9 Christian Festivals

The Christian Church keeps a number of festivals throughout the year. The calendar begins with the season of Advent in November, four weeks before Christmas Day. The principal festival occasions are:

Advent:	preparation for the coming of Jesus Christ—November or December (the fourth Sunday before Christmas)
Christmas:	the commemoration of Jesus' birth—25th December
Epiphany:	the visit of the Wise Men to the Infant Jesus—6th January
Lent:	the forty days before Easter (ending at midnight before Easter Day)
Shrove Tuesday:	also called Pancake Tuesday; the last day before Lent
Ash Wednesday:	the first day of Lent— March or April
Palm Sunday:	Jesus' entry into Jerusalem—the Sunday before Easter
Maundy Thursday:	the day of the Last Supper on which Jesus commanded the disciples to love one another
Good Friday:	the crucifixion of Jesus
Easter Day:	the resurrection of Jesus

(The above four celebrations fall in one week, Holy Week, in March or April and make up the Easter festival.)

Ascension Day:	Jesus' ascension into Heaven—April or May (the Thursday forty days after Easter Day)
Whitsun or Pentecost:	the gift of the Holy Spirit to the Apostles— May or June (the seventh Sunday or fifty days after Easter)
Trinity Sunday:	A remembrance of the doctrine of the Trinity—May or June (the Sunday after Whitsun)

The whole Christian year revolves around the historical events in the life of Jesus and events concerning the early Church and its teaching. All these festivals are celebrated in church with special services when the appropriate Bible lessons and prayers are used and suitable hymns are sung. Also sermons are preached which have themes fitting the occasion.

Advent
The word 'Advent' means 'coming', and it reminds Christians of two important beliefs:

firstly the Incarnation (meaning 'in the flesh') which is the coming of Jesus Christ, the Son of God, on earth as a man, and secondly the Second Coming of Christ in Glory when he will judge mankind. Generally it is a period of preparation for the celebration of Jesus' birth on earth. Special Advent candles are lit and children are given Advent calendars. On these calendars children mark off the days of Advent as they pass. In some European countries the festival of St Nicholas is celebrated on 6th December. The children especially receive presents which are often left somewhere in the house secretly. Younger children believe that St Nicholas himself delivers them! This recalls how St Nicholas, who lived in Myra (in Turkey) in the 4th century, secretly helped the poor by leaving gifts of food and fuel on their doorstep at night.

Christmas

The celebration of Christmas has been held by the Church for centuries No one knows the exact date of Jesus' birth. In pagan religions there were a number of festivals around this time in late December, especially concerning the sun. The Church therefore decided on 25th December as a suitable day to celebrate the birth of Jesus. It meant that Christian people would not feel neglected at a time when everyone else was enjoying themselves. Many of the customs associated with Christmas are not, therefore, specifically Christian in origin.

The key message of Christmas is that God sent His Son to Earth as a man to bring the message of light and love to mankind. So Christmas is a time of goodwill when not only practising Christians try to be as kind and considerate as they can. Family re-

A nativity crib scene

unions are held, presents are exchanged, and Christmas cards are sent with suitable greetings. It is a particularly happy time for children. In Britain Father Christmas or Santa Claus (St Nicholas) brings presents on Christmas Eve in the same way as he does in other countries on St Nicholas' Day.

Many people decorate their homes with paper chains and tinsel. In former days, evergreens, particularly holly and ivy were used. Most homes have a decorated Christmas tree. In the past candles were put on the tree, but nowadays coloured lights are usually used. These are a symbol of Jesus as the Light of the World, and the evergreens symbolize life since they do not shed their leaves in winter. By tradition, St Boniface first chose the Christmas tree for decoration since he said its pointed shape reminded people of the way to heaven (just like a church spire).

A decorated Christmas tree

In every church there are special services held throughout the festival. A service of Nine Lessons and Carols which retell the birth of Jesus and the meaning of His life is a particular favourite. Generally the singing of Christmas carols is very popular. Many churches have a nativity crib scene on display. It depicts Mary and Joseph in the stable with the Infant Jesus in the manger sur-

rounded by the animals, the shepherds and the Three Wise Men with their gifts.

Many special foods are prepared for the Christmas season. These include Christmas cake (a rich iced fruit cake), mince pies (pastry pies with a sweet filling) which are a symbol of Jesus' manger, and a Yule Log (a chocolate-coated sponge cake). On Christmas Day itself families enjoy a traditional dinner of turkey and stuffing, followed by a special fruit pudding. Often silver coins are put in the pudding to surprise the lucky finders. These puddings are often round in shape, and before being eaten, brandy is poured over and set alight! Some say this is a reminder of the festival's very early association with the pagan worship of the sun.

Lent
Throughout Lent, that is the forty days leading up to Easter Day, there are a number of important feast days.

Shrove Tuesday
This day is sometimes called Pancake Day because during Lent certain foods were forbidden, and so housewives finished up all the fat and cream left in the house in a pancake. However the day has a more serious significance. In the past, all Christians confessed their sins to a priest and asked for forgiveness. The priest responded by offering God's forgiveness and by imposing a penance. This is called 'being shriven' (from an old English word), from which the word 'shrove' comes. Since this day was the last opportunity for enjoyment for several weeks, many entertainments took place. These included street football matches, tug-of-war competitions and pancake races. Some of these events are still held today.

Ash Wednesday
This day derives its name from an old custom of a sinner appearing in public wearing sackcloth and ashes. Nowadays in some churches palm crosses which were presented the year before are burned and the ashes are used to mark a cross on the forehead.

A palm Sunday procession in Spain

Palm Sunday

This is the first day of Holy Week and it commemorates Jesus riding into Jerusalem on a donkey, when the people welcomed Him by waving palm branches. Many churches hold special processions when the people carry palm branches, and they are given small crosses made from strips of folded palm leaves. Other churches have special services during which they hold dramatic readings of the last week of Jesus' life which is known as 'the Passion'.

Maundy Thursday

On this day Jesus ate the Last Supper with His Disciples. He also gave them a new commandment, and as He did so, He washed their feet. This act of humility and service symbolized the commandment, which instructed His disciples to love one another as He loved them. The word 'Maundy' comes from a Latin word 'mandatum' which means 'commandment'. For many years services were held on this day at which the priest washed the feet of some of his parishioners. Even today the Pope often performs the same duty by washing the feet of some of the poor in Rome. British monarchs used to do the same, but about 200 years ago it was replaced by the distribution of the Royal Maundy Money. This custom still continues today when the money is given to a number of old-age pensioners at a special service. The number of coins is always the same as the age of the monarch.

Good Friday

This day is sometimes known as 'Black Friday'. It is a very solemn day commemorating the death of Jesus on the Cross. Usually churches are left undecorated, there are no flowers and no cloths on the altar. The services concentrate on the events of Good Friday and some churches have readings of the Gospel account of Jesus' Crucifixion with appropriate prayers and music. Christians are reminded that, although Jesus suffered and died on this day, out of those cruel events came hope. Jesus faced the challenge of evil and successfully overcame mankind's sin, since after three days God raised him to life. By dying, Christians believe that Jesus made it possible for anyone who believes in him to be delivered from their sin.

Hot Cross buns are eaten on Good Friday. They are sweet and contain currants and spices, and the marking of the cross on them is a reminder of the crucifixion. Originally they were intended to break the Lenten fast.

Easter Day

Easter derives its name from Eastre or Eostre, the Goddess of Spring. The whole theme of Easter is one of new life since on that day Christians celebrate the resurrection of Jesus from the dead. For Christians this festival is the most important in the year. The churches are always beautifully decorated with spring flowers, and in some a miniature Easter Garden is put on display. This is a model of the Hill of Calvary where Jesus was crucified with its three crosses, and the Garden of the Resurrection with its empty tomb.

Most churches have a special service of Holy Communion on Easter Day which is always well attended. Many churches welcome Easter with a service at midnight where the Paschal candle is the focal point. This candle has five grains of incense inserted in the form of a cross, and it burns in the church until Ascension Day, forty days later.

It is a custom to give eggs as presents since they are a symbol of new life. Sometimes they are chocolate eggs filled with sweets. Many people hard-boil ordinary eggs and then dye them or decorate them. In some parts of the country children roll these eggs down a slope and the one that rolls the farthest wins a prize. This signifies the rolling away of the stone from the tomb.

In the north-east of England children play a game called 'jarping'. Hard-boiled eggs are banged together as in a game of 'conkers', and the winner is the one whose egg lasts as long as possible without breaking.

Whitsun

On this day the Church celebrates the coming of the Holy Spirit into the Apostles after Jesus had ascended into heaven. This event had such an effect on the Apostles that they lost their fear of the Jewish authorities and they began to preach the Gospel in Jerusalem. Within a short time many more people had become followers of Jesus. It is for this reason that this festival may be called the Birthday of the Church. It is also called Pentecost, a Greek word meaning 'fiftieth' for the fifty days after Easter.

This was always a popular time for people to be baptized as Christians. White clothes were worn as a sign of new life and purity. As a result, this day became known as White Sunday, which in time became Whitsunday.

Trinity Sunday

This takes place eight weeks after Easter in May or June. As with other festivals, special services are held in church. On this day Christians remember the teaching of God as the Holy Trinity. 'Trinity' means 'Three in One' and it reminds Christians of the doctrine that there are three persons in one God, i.e. the Father, the Son and the Holy Spirit. Trinity Sunday is also an occasion for the ordination of priests or deacons after their training has been completed. They then begin working in the Church.

In addition to the festivals there are many saints commemorated by the Church. In fact the Book of Common Prayer lists over seventy but not all have appointed 'days'. An important one, however, is All Saints Day on 1st November which remembers all Christian saints, known or not. Many churches are dedicated to a particular saint and hold a festival on their particular saint's day. The patron saints are remembered in each part of Britain as follows:

1st March:	St David (Wales)
17th March:	St Patrick (Ireland)
23rd April:	St George (England)
30th November:	St Andrew (Scotland)

Most countries of the world and some cities also have their patron saints.

Glossary

Advent	beginning of the Christian Year in November and December; a period of preparation for the celebration of Jesus' coming at Christmas (cf. page 19)
Altar	a stone or wooden table in church round which Mass or Holy Communion is celebrated (cf. page 8)
Anglican	member of the Church of England (cf. page 17)
Apostles	same as **Disciples**
Ascension	festival commemorating Jesus' return to heaven after His Resurrection (cf. page 19)
Ash Wednesday	first day of the season of Lent (cf. page 19)
Baptism	ceremony in church when infants (or in the Baptist Church, adults) are blessed and given a name (cf. page 4)
Belfry	part of the church tower containing the bells (cf. page 7)
Bible	book containing the sacred writings of the Christian faith (cf. page 14)
Cathedra	bishop's throne in a cathedral (cf. page 10)
Cathedral	main church of a diocese containing the bishop's throne (cf. page 10)
Chalice	silver cup containing the wine used in Mass or Holy Communion (cf. page 11)
Chancel	eastern end of a church where the choir and sanctuary are situated (cf. page 8)
Christmas	festival commemorating the birth of Jesus held on 25th December (cf. page 19)
Church	the Christian place of worship (cf. page 7)
Clergy	body of people who have been ordained to be ministers in the Church (cf. page 8)
Confirmation	ceremony at which a person is received into membership of the Church (cf. page 5)
Creed	statement which sets out the main beliefs of the Church (cf. page 13)
Cremation	burning of the dead; used in place of burial (cf. page 7)
Crematorium	building at which cremation takes place (cf. page 7)
Crucifix	image of Jesus on the Cross or the cross itself (cf. page 13)
Disciples	followers of Jesus; 'the twelve disciples'—the twelve men chosen by Jesus to be His close companions (cf. page 2)
Easter	festival celebrating Jesus' Resurrection (cf. page 19)
Epiphany	twelfth day after Christmas celebrating the visit of the Wise Men to the Infant Jesus (cf. page 19)
Font	basin containing the water used in the baptism ceremony in Church (cf. page 4)
Good Friday	day when Christians remember the Crucifixion of Jesus (cf. page 19)

Gospel	means 'Good News'; name of the first four books in the New Testament narrating the life and teaching of Jesus (cf. page 15)
Hymns	sacred songs used in Christian worship (cf. page 10)
Incarnation	Christian doctrine that God appeared on earth as a man in the person of Jesus (cf. page 20)
Judas Iscariot	disciple of Jesus who betrayed him to the Jewish authorities (cf. page 2)
Laying-on of Hands	action of placing the hands on a person's head performed by a bishop during confirmation; it is believed the action bestows the Holy Spirit (cf. page 6)
Lectern	stand in church on which the Bible is placed and from which passages are read aloud (cf. page 8)
Lent	period of forty days in Spring leading up to Easter during which Christians prepare to celebrate the death and resurrection of Jesus (cf. page 19)
Lesson	passage from the Bible read aloud during worship (cf. page 15)
Matins	form of worship in the morning in the Church of England (cf. page 11)
Maundy Thursday	Thursday during Holy Week before Easter Day (cf. page 19)
Messiah	expected ruler whom the Jews believed would deliver them from their enemies (cf. page 2)
Nave	central section of a church where the congregation sits (cf. page 8)
Palm Sunday	Sunday before Easter Day when Christians remember Jesus riding into Jerusalem on a donkey (cf. page 19)
Pentecost	same as **Whitsun**
Pews	seats in the nave of a church (cf. page 8)
Psalms	sacred songs used in worship and found in the Old Testament (cf. page 10)
Pulpit	raised, enclosed platform from which sermons are preached in church (cf. page 8)
Rosary	string of beads used by Christians as an aid in prayer (cf. page 13)
Sanctuary	part of a church containing the altar (cf. page 8)
Service	public worship when a particular form is used, e.g. Mass, Matins, etc. (cf. page 10)
Sunday	first day of the week; the holy day of the Christian Church (cf. page 10)
Testament	either of the two main parts of the Bible, i.e. Old Testament or New Testament (cf. page 14)
Trinity Sunday	day when Christians remember the doctrine that there is One God in Three Persons: Father, Son and Holy Spirit (cf. page 19)
Whitsun	festival celebrating the coming of the Holy Spirit on the followers of Jesus after His Resurrection (cf. page 19)

·Activities·

1 Important Things to Remember and Understand

Special words and ideas: Advent; Ascension; baptism; creed; crucifix; Incarnation; laying-on of hands; Messiah.

2 Important Things to Find Out

Festivals are very important in Christianity. Find out how your local churches celebrate these occasions.

Find out about famous Christians, past and present, who, because of their Christian beliefs, have worked to improve life in general.

Ask a person who has just accepted the Christian faith how it came about and what difference it has made to their life.

3 Important Things to Discuss

Christians are just people who go around trying to do good. Is this a fair statement? Discuss the teaching of Jesus, particularly what he said in the Sermon on the Mount. 'The Church should stick to saving people's souls and not get mixed up in politics.' Discuss this statement.

4 Important Things to Do

Visit a local church to learn about the work of the priest (or minister) and how the church serves the local community.

Make some posters illustrating the festivals in the Christian year.

Find out about different types of crosses and make a chart of them.

5 Written Work

a Describe and comment on the stages a person must undergo to become a member of the Christian Church.

b Imagine you are visiting a particular church and explain what features you see and their purpose. How is a cathedral different from a church?

c Explain to a non-Christian what the Bible is and how Christians use the book in worship.

CHAPTER 2

· Judaism ·

1 What is Judaism?

Judaism is the name of the religion of the Jews. The name comes from Judah, the eldest son of Jacob, who was one of the patriarchs of the early Jews. The descendants of Judah came to Palestine with the other tribes after they had been released from slavery in Egypt by Moses (see page 29). These tribes were known as the Children of Israel, which was Jacob's other name.

At the beginning of the 10th century BC, the descendants of the Children of Israel in Palestine were ruled by King David who had united the people into one strong kingdom called Israel. However, by the end of the century it had split up into two kingdoms—Israel in the north and Judah in the south. In the 8th century the northern kingdom of Israel disappeared when it was conquered by the Assyrians and made part of their em-

pire. However, the Kingdom of Judah kept its independence until 586 BC when the Babylonians took over the country and transported most of the people into exile in Babylon. Yet the people of Judah retained their identity, and when they were allowed to return to their homeland some fifty years later, their religion and culture were intact since they had taken great care to preserve them. It is from these people of Judah that the Jews of today are descended.

Nowadays, by tradition, only a person who has a Jewish mother is a Jew. However more progressive Jews say that a Jew is anyone who has either a Jewish mother or a Jewish father, and who has been brought up as a Jew. Furthermore by following a period of instruction before being admitted to a synagogue anyone can become a Jew.

2 The Patriarchs

The beginnings of the Jewish faith can be traced back to the Patriarchs whom the Jews regard as the 'Fathers' of their religion. These 'Fathers' were Abraham, Isaac and Jacob; of these the most important is Abraham.

Abraham
Abraham lived in the city of Ur in about 2000 BC. This city was situated on the banks of the River Euphrates, which today runs through the modern state of Iraq. At some

point in his life Abraham left Ur with his family and migrated north-westwards up the valley of the Euphrates to the city of Haran.

Abraham did not stay long in Haran. Within a few years he had set off for a new life in Canaan (which was later called Palestine). He was quite sure that God had called him to do this. The Jewish scriptures describe how a covenant or agreement was made between Abraham and God. God told Abraham to leave his homeland and journey

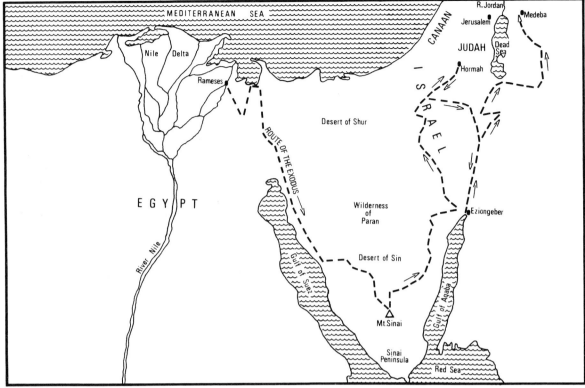

The route taken by Moses and the Children of Israel to the Promised Land

to a land 'which I will show you'. God also told Abraham that he would be the father of a great nation and his descendants would possess this new land for ever. In return Abraham agreed to serve God always and worship only Him. Abraham with his family remained in Canaan, but his life was mainly that of a wandering nomad. (At this time Abraham and his tribe were called 'the Hebrews'.) The covenant between Abraham and God was renewed with Isaac, his son, and Jacob, his grandson. When Jacob renewed the promises with God he was given the additional name 'Israel'. This is why later on his descendants were called the Children of Israel.

Moses

The next great figure to play an important part in the formation of the Jewish faith was Moses. During the life of Jacob the early Jews settled in Egypt at the invitation of the Egyptian rulers. For several generations they lived there peaceably and untroubled. However, when a new line of kings came to

power in Egypt, life changed dramatically for Jacob's descendants (now called the Children of Israel or the Israelites). The new king or Pharaoh became very suspicious of the Israelites and eventually they were forced into slavery. It was into this situation that Moses was born.

Moses was born in Egypt to Israelite parents in about 1300 BC. At that time the Pharaoh ordered all the male infants of the Israelites to be killed at birth. According to the Book of Exodus in the Bible Moses' life was saved and he was brought up by an Egyptian princess as a royal prince. As a young man, although he lived a life of luxury, he never forgot his own people, the Israelites. On one occasion, when defending one of his fellow countrymen, he unintentionally killed an Egyptian slave driver, and he was forced to flee from Egypt to save his life.

Moses settled in the desert around Mount Sinai where he lived with a group of herdsmen, one of whose daughters he later married. Here on the slopes of the mountain he had a tremendous experience which changed his whole life. In this incident, known as 'the story of the Burning Bush', God revealed himself to Moses and told him that He had chosen him to lead His people, the Children of Israel, from their suffering in Egypt. He was to take them back to Canaan, the land promised to Abraham's descendants.

Moses accepted this new task with some reluctance and returned to Egypt. The Pharaoh was unwilling to free such valuable slaves, and not even a succession of disasters, which Moses said God had sent down on the Egyptians, would change his mind. Only the final disaster when all the first-born sons of the Egyptians, including the Pharaoh's heir, were struck down by a fatal disease, persuaded the Pharaoh to release the slaves. Moses immediately led the Children of Israel out of Egypt and across the Red Sea into the desert around Mount Sinai. Even then the Pharaoh changed his mind and he sent his army after the Israelites to bring them back, but it was destroyed when crossing the Red Sea. So the Children of Israel, after much suffering, regained their freedom at last.

Moses led the people through the desert to the foot of Mount Sinai where they made camp. He then climbed the mountain to communicate with God and when he returned the old covenant was renewed, but this time it was between God and His people. It meant that the people accepted God as their Guide and Protector, and promised to obey Him faithfully. They came to believe that God had especially chosen them to be His people and that through them the world would come to know Him and learn to live in peace and unity. The covenant was sealed in a solemn ceremony involving the offering of sacrifices; half the blood from the sacrifices was sprinkled on the altar for God, and the other half over the people.

At this time Moses gave God's Law, which he had received when he ascended Mount Sinai, to the people; the basis of this was the Ten Commandments. The Law aimed to raise the level of the religious and

Moses—depicted by Gustav Doré

moral life of the people. He also appointed Elders (judges) from each of the twelve tribes of the Israelites to help him to administer the Law. It says in the Book of Exodus that the Ten Commandments were engraved on stone tablets which were then placed in the Ark. The Ark was a large box which was carried by priests on behalf of the people as they journeyed through the desert. Eventually it was placed in the Temple built by King Solomon in Jerusalem.

For some forty years Moses led the Children of Israel in their wanderings in the desert. During this time the Twelve Tribes of the Children of Israel were moulded into a nation which eventually was strong enough to march into the Promised Land (Canaan) and settle there. Moses himself did not enter Canaan; his task was finished when he brought them to the borders of the country, and there he died. It was left to his successor, Joshua, to take the people across the River Jordan into Canaan itself. Moses played an enormous part in the establishment of the Jewish faith; even today Jews say there has been no prophet greater than him. As it says in one of the Thirteen Articles of the Jewish faith 'I believe that the prophecy of Moses, our teacher, was true, and that he was the chief of the prophets'.

3 The Synagogue

The Jewish place of worship is called the synagogue which means 'a gathering', hence 'a place or house of assembly'. It is the building where Jews meet to worship God and to study His Law.

The first synagogues were built when the Jews were in exile in Babylon in the 6th century BC. The prophet Ezekiel encouraged the Jews to build synagogues to help them to preserve their faith during this captivity. On their return to Israel synagogues became the local centres of worship in the towns and villages. After the destruction of the Temple in AD 70 by the Romans, synagogues became vital institutions for the preservation of the Jewish faith.

A synagogue with the menorah depicted on its gates

Synagogues are not required to be built in any particular shape or style but they are usually rectangular. The side of a synagogue which is the focal point always faces Jerusalem, the holy city of the Jews, so that worshippers face in that direction. The 'Shield or Star of David' symbol on the outside wall may be the only indication that the building is a synagogue. As can be seen at the start of the chapter, the symbol consists of two interlocking triangles. It seems to have originated in antiquity as a magical sign. It is not clear how the symbol became associated with King David. One suggestion is that the star represented a bow which David used as a shield. Another is that the

star was really the capital letter D since an old Hebrew form of this was made in the shape of a triangle. It has also been said by Franz Rosenschweig that the six points of the star stand for God, the world, man, and God's great acts of Creation, Revelation and Redemption. It has been generally used as a symbol of Judaism since the 17th century. Nowadays the modern state of Israel also uses it as its national symbol.

Inside a Synagogue

The main features inside are the ark and bimah.

The ark is a decorated cabinet or cupboard and, as it is the focal point of the synagogue, it is placed in the centre of the main wall. It contains the scrolls on which the Jewish Law, the Torah, is written. When its doors are shut they are covered by a curtain. Above the ark are two tablets on which are written in Hebrew the first words of the Ten Commandments. Below these are the words, again in Hebrew, 'Know before whom you stand'.

The scrolls are long pieces of parchment, on wooden rollers, on which the Torah is written. On the end of the rollers are silver ornaments and bells, and often there is a silver crown since the Torah is called 'the

The ark, with curtains drawn and the tablets above

crown of life'. The scrolls are covered with mantles of velvet, silk or brocade which are richly decorated with religious symbols. Over the mantle is a silver breastplate which reminds the Jews of the one worn by the High Priest in the Temple in Jerusalem. It had twelve precious stones embedded in it representing the Twelve Tribes of Israel.

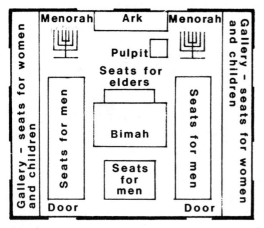

A plan of a synagogue

The menorah is a large candlestick with seven branches. There are usually two of these in the synagogue which are placed near the ark, one on each side. They are a reminder of the large candlesticks that were in the Temple. Near the ark, hanging from the ceiling, is a lamp. This reminds Jews of the light that burned continually in the Temple, and of the presence of God and the Torah.

In front of the ark is a pulpit which is used by the Rabbi or preacher when he addresses the congregation. The bimah, a raised platform with rails, stands in the centre of the

synagogue where all the congregation can see it. On the bimah is a reading desk on which the scrolls are placed when they are read out aloud during worship.

There are special seats positioned next to the bimah. They face the ark and are reserved for the Elders of the synagogue. These men organize worship in the synagogue and govern its affairs. The seating for the congregation is arranged so that everyone can see the bimah easily. Usually the women and the children sit upstairs in a gallery while the men occupy the seats downstairs.

Some synagogues are beautiful inside with richly decorated columns, walls and stained-glass windows. However the Jewish Law forbids pictures or statues, but there may be quotations in Hebrew written on the walls. Other synagogues are very plain inside. Often it depends how much the congregation can afford to spend on their synagogue.

The interior of a synagogue

4 Jewish Worship

The Sabbath: the Jewish Holy Day
Saturday, the last day of the week, is the Jewish holy day. The day is called the Sabbath, a word which means 'rest'. This reminds Jews of their teaching that God created the Universe in six days, and then

rested on the seventh day. The Sabbath begins at sunset on Friday and lasts until sunset on Saturday. Since sunset in Israel is at 6 p.m. the Sabbath everywhere begins at 6 p.m. on Friday and ends twenty-four hours later.

For Jews the Sabbath is a day of great joy, and the most important day of the week. It is the time, particularly set apart from the rest of the week, for special worship and thanksgiving to God. Furthermore, it is a day of relaxation and recreation free from worry when everyone is refreshed in readiness for the coming week.

Ceremonies at Home on the Sabbath

Before the Sabbath begins the Jewish housewife cleans the house and prepares the Sabbath meal. The men go to the synagogue at the beginning of the Sabbath. At home the table is laid by the housewife ready for the evening meal. As dusk falls she welcomes the beginning of the Sabbath with the children by lighting some candles and saying a blessing.

The Evening Ceremony

When the husband returns home from the synagogue he gathers the family round the table for what is called the Kiddush ceremony. He prays for his children and blesses them. He then reads the last twenty-two verses of the Book of Proverbs (see page 39) which are a tribute to all Jewish wives and mothers.

Next he recites the Kiddush, the prayer of sanctification, over a glass of wine. This tells everyone that the Sabbath is set apart as a special day and it reminds everyone of

God's kindness. Then everyone present drinks a little of the wine. On the table are two specially baked loaves of bread covered with a cloth. They are a reminder that God sent the Children of Israel manna (a kind of bread) when they were in the desert with Moses, and on the Sabbath they received a double portion, so that they should not work on that day. The husband takes the bread, blesses it, then hands it round to all the members of the family.

The family then eats the meal which the housewife has prepared. At the end of the meal the husband washes his hands in a bowl of water, and everyone joins in singing special Sabbath songs. The celebration closes with the recitation of the Grace, in which God is remembered for providing His children with food, and for His loving kindness and mercy.

The Sabbath ends on the Saturday evening with another ceremony conducted by the husband with the help of his son. Some candles are lit and the husband says the Havdalah prayer to mark the separation of the Sabbath from the other days of the week. He then says two blessings; the first over a glass of wine, and the second over a box containing spices. The box is passed to each member of the family in turn so that they can smell the fragrance. This is to symbolize the hope that the fragrance of the Sabbath will continue throughout the coming week. Finally, a blessing is spoken over the lighted candles, and they are extinguished.

At Worship

When Jewish men (including boys over the age of thirteen) pray and worship God they wear a yarmulka, a tallith and tefillin (also called phylacteries). Each of these has a special significance and aids them in their worship. The yarmulka is a small embroidered skull cap which is worn as a sign of respect. The tallith is a rectangular prayer shawl which is white in colour with tassels and fringes at each end. There are also black or blue stripes across the ends. The tassels are made up of 613 strands and knots which is the number of the regulations in the Torah,

The Kiddush ceremony

and they remind Jews to observe God's Law all the time. The tefillin are leather boxes with long leather thongs attached to them. They contain small scrolls on which are written short passages from the Torah. One box is fastened on the forehead (i.e. nearest the mind) and the other on the left forearm (i.e. nearest the heart). The Shema, one of the ancient Jewish prayers (see page 39), instructs Jews to wear the tefillin and put up a mezuzah (see page 38).

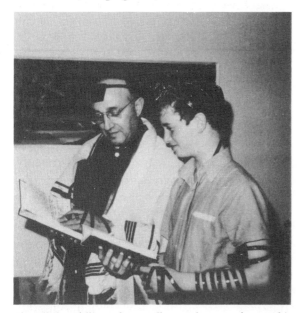

The tallith, tefellin and yarmulka are also worn for worship at home

There are two officials who play an important part in synagogue worship. The first is the Rabbi (meaning 'teacher') who is the leader of the Jews in the local community. He is an expert in the Jewish Law, therefore he can deal with any matters connected with it and give advice when requested. He will often preach during synagogue worship; usually he explains the passages that have been read out from the Torah. The other official is the Cantor or Reader. He leads the service in the synagogue. He must have a good voice as most of the service is chanted.

According to Jewish Law before worship can take place in the synagogue there must be ten males present over the age of thirteen years. This group is called the minyan.

The Sabbath Service

In the Orthodox synagogues the service on the Sabbath lasts about two hours. The men sit downstairs wearing their skull caps (though other hats are allowed) and talliths. Before and after putting on the tallith a prayer is spoken. A prayer book is also needed during the service. Usually when entering the synagogue the people say 'as for me, in the abundance of Thy loving kindness will I come into Thy house'. They bow to the ark as it contains the Word of God. The Cantor enters wearing a black gown, a hat and a white scarf, and he takes his place on the bimah.

The service begins with the reading of a number of Psalms from the Prayer Book. Any man can lead the reading; everyone in the congregation reads the passages at the same time. The Cantor then sings passages which tell how God has saved his people many times in the past and the section ends with the Cantor reciting the Shema. There follows the saying of the Amidah, a prayer which everyone offers silently while standing facing the ark.

At this point in the service the most important part takes place, that is the opening of the ark and the reading of the Torah. The

The open ark, showing the scrolls on which the Torah is written

Elders of the synagogue, along with two members of the congregation, whom they have invited, go to the ark and take out the scrolls. These are carried in procession to the bimah. As they pass, the men try to touch the scrolls with their talliths. Once on the bimah the scrolls are held up for all to see, and blessings are spoken over them. The men take turns to read the Torah. It is a great honour to be asked to read. While reading, the men point to each word with a silver pointer made in the shape of a finger. When the reading is completed the people stand and say, 'This is the Law which Moses set before the Children of Israel'. Again the scrolls are held up for the people to see and

more blessings are spoken. They are then returned to the ark in procession.

To complete the service a number of prayers are spoken: first the Amidah, this time spoken by the Cantor, then the Kaddish for those in mourning for the departed members of the family (see 'Death' page 36). The Alenu prayer follows, and finally the Hymn of Glory chanted by the Cantor or occasionally by a young child.

There are no offerings of money made in synagogue worship on the Sabbath as the Torah forbids the exchange of money on the holy day. Usually all Jews give a regular fixed offering of money to the synagogue each week.

5 Jewish Initiation and Other Important Ceremonies

Birth Ceremonies

Shortly after the birth of a baby boy, on the eighth day, an important ceremony takes place. This is circumcision or the cutting of the foreskin of a baby boy. The ceremony takes place in the synagogue or in the child's home, and it is performed by the Rabbi. Prayers are said for the health of the baby and its mother, and the baby is given its name. One of the important prayers offered is, 'Even as this child has entered into the Covenant, so may he enter into the Torah, the marriage canopy and into good deeds.'

For Jews, circumcision is of great religious significance. It is a sign in the flesh of God's covenant with Abraham when He promised to make him the father of a great nation. It is also a constant reminder to a Jew of his great religious heritage.

A ceremony is also performed in the synagogue to name baby girls. The parents bring their child to the synagogue and the father is called to a public reading of the Torah from the scroll. Special prayers are said for the welfare of the mother and child, and for the child to be strong and healthy, and to hold fast to the Jewish faith. The parents are blessed, and the name of the baby is announced.

Bar-Mitzvah

When a Jewish boy reaches the age of thirteen he goes through a special ceremony in the synagogue called bar-mitzvah (this means 'Son of the Commandment'). Before the ceremony takes place the boy must attend a course of instruction conducted by the Rabbi so that he can understand Hebrew, the language of Jewish sacred writings. He also studies the Jewish religious law so that he gains a thorough knowledge of its content.

The ceremony takes place on the Sabbath nearest to the boy's thirteenth birthday. It begins with the prayers and readings of a usual synagogue service. The scrolls of the Law are taken out of the ark and prepared for reading, then the boy is called out by name to the bimah. He takes his place alongside the men, one of whom is his father, whose task is to read passages of the Law aloud. After the men have read their portion of the Law, the Rabbi invites the boy to read in Hebrew special sections from the books of Genesis and Isaiah. After this the Rabbi preaches a sermon, part of which he addresses to the boy. He reminds him that he is now a full member of the Jewish community and it is his duty to observe the Jewish Law

A bar-mitzvah ceremony

to the best of his ability. From that time on he is treated as an adult, and it is his responsibility to keep the commandments throughout his daily life. Finally the boy is blessed with a benediction which begins, 'The Lord bless thee and keep thee'.

Following the ceremony the boy's parents give a party for all his relations and friends to celebrate the day. It is a very happy occasion; the boy is given presents and he makes a speech in which he thanks his parents and the Rabbi for guiding him as he grew up in the faith, and he thanks his relations and friends for their presents.

There is a similar ceremony for girls, but it takes place earlier when they are twelve years of age. Their ceremony is called bat-mitzvah, which means 'daughter of the Commandment'. It has the same significance as bar-mitzvah, and means that girls begin their religious duties a year before Jewish boys.

A Jewish Wedding

The Jewish wedding ceremony is called 'Kiddhushin' which means 'to be holy'. To the Jews, marriage is a holy thing which was instituted by God, and it reminds them that the home is a sanctuary in which God dwells for ever.

The marriage ceremony takes place in the synagogue, and it is conducted by the Cantor and the Rabbi. Before the ceremony begins a velvet canopy supported by four poles is erected before the ark.

The bridegroom stands with his father under the canopy awaiting his bride. When the bride arrives she joins the bridegroom under the canopy whilst the Cantor sings a welcome. With their parents standing alongside the bride and groom, and with the bridesmaid(s) and the best man behind, the Rabbi talks to the couple about marriage. He tells them that the canopy is a symbol of their future home and it is their duty to keep their home holy.

The Rabbi then chants the 'Blessing of Betrothal' over a glass of wine, and the bride and groom each take a sip of the wine. The groom then places a ring on the bride's finger while he promises to honour her

A Jewish wedding ceremony

all his life. The Rabbi reads part of the marriage contract, the Ketubah, which the groom has signed, and in which he promises to be a true and faithful husband.

An extract from a Hebrew wedding contract

When this reading is over, the Cantor chants the Seven Blessings, which praise God for his acts of creation, over a glass of wine. Then the glass is put on the floor, and the groom breaks it with his foot as the congregation shouts 'Good Luck! Congratulations!'. This action reminds the couple, first, not to forget their responsibilities on this joyful occasion, and, second, of the destruction of the Temple in Jerusalem, which the Jewish people should never forget.

The bride and groom are now man and wife, and the service ends with a benediction beginning 'The Lord bless thee and keep thee'. As with all weddings, the proceedings end with a reception and banquet to which all the couple's relations and friends are invited.

Death

When a Jew dies, the body is prepared for burial by being washed and wrapped in a clean white linen shroud. This is often done by the most respected members of the Jewish community. The body is then placed in a simple coffin made from plain wood. At the burial in the cemetery prayers are said and the nearest relatives each shovel some earth into the grave.

For the next seven days following a burial the mourners stay at home, and, as a sign of grief, they sit on low stools. They wear no leather shoes, and all mirrors in the house are covered. Whenever visitors come to the house to offer sympathy and comfort, they recite prayers for the soul of the dead person. All Jews consider it their duty to visit the bereaved.

For the next twelve months following the death of a parent, a son attends worship in the synagogue and recites aloud the mourner's prayer known as Kaddish. 'Kaddish' means 'holiness' since the prayer is a plea for God's holiness to be felt by all men. Each year on the anniversary of a parent's death, the son also recites the prayer, and the family keeps a light burning throughout the day, since in the Jewish scriptures a man's soul is compared to a light set ablaze by God. Thereafter the graves of parents are visited regularly and at least once a year.

6 Daily Religious Observances

Every devout Jew carries out various religious practices each day. The most important of these is prayer. Others concern their food, and the remembrance of God's Law with the aid of a small religious object called a mezuzah.

Prayer

Regular and frequent prayer is an essential part of Jewish daily life. Jews may pray whenever they wish, but for the men there are three set occasions for prayer, i.e. morning, noon and evening, which may be carried out in the home or in the synagogue. At these special prayer times a Jew wears his skull cap, his tallith and his tefillin. There are no set times for women concerning prayer; they pray whenever it is convenient during the day.

A devout Jew makes careful preparations before praying. For instance in the morning he first washes his hands, then offers prayers of thanksgiving to God for a new day. He always washes before eating any food and says prayers before and after meals.

The morning service of prayer in the synagogue includes blessings, prayers and meditation. In the prayers there are references to honouring parents, giving help to those in need, attending the synagogue regularly and visiting the sick. In the service the Amidah, Psalms, the Kaddish and the Alenu prayers are recited.

The Amidah is a series of eighteen benedictions. They include praise to God, thanks to Him for His goodness and petitions to God. The contents of the Amidah vary according to the occasion, but the first three and the last three benedictions are always the same. It includes such passages as 'Let the words of my mouth and the meditation of my heart be acceptable before thee, O Lord and my Redeemer'.

The Psalms are used in all acts of worship. Some psalms are linked with particular days, e.g. no. 24 for Sunday, 40 for Monday, 92 for the Sabbath. Psalm 145 is one of praise and it is repeated several times during daily worship. It begins 'I will praise thee, my God, O King; and I will bless thy name for ever and ever. Every day will I bless thee, and I will praise thy name for ever and ever'.

The Kaddish prayer is spoken in three daily services. 'Kaddish', meaning 'sanctification', is linked with the setting up of God's Kingdom on Earth, with the hope of peace and brotherhood throughout the world, and with the belief that all who have died will enjoy everlasting life.

The Alenu prayer, also recited in daily prayers, declares that God is the King over Israel, and all the Universe, and that all men should recognize Him as Lord.

If a Jew does not attend the daily prayers in the synagogue, he is required to observe the prayer-time at home. He may use the prayers printed in the Prayer Book or he may offer extempore prayers, i.e. those which are 'made up' as he speaks. He always says particular prayers before putting on the tallith and as he fastens on the tefillin. Each prayer directs his mind towards God and helps him to meditate on God's purpose for men.

The order of service is written in the Prayer Book or Siddur (meaning 'order'). The original Siddur consisted of the Psalms of David, but over the centuries additional prayers were included, so that the version that is used today contains all that is necessary for daily prayers and worship. The prayer book used by most Jewish congregations in Great Britain is the Authorized Daily Prayer Book, which was first used in 1890. Since then it has been revised several times under the guidance of the Chief Rabbi.

Jewish Food Laws

Some of the most important religious laws which Jews must keep concern food. Usually it is the responsibility of the Jewish housewife to ensure that the laws are observed. Jews may only eat food that has been prepared according to the Law: such food is called Kosher. Jewish housewives always buy food from Jewish shops where they know that all the food on sale has been prepared in the correct way.

Jews may only eat meat from animals which have cloven hooves and which chew the cud, e.g. cattle and sheep, and flesh from fish that have fins and scales. Products from birds of prey and from birds that have not been slaughtered in the required way may not be eaten. In fact any meat must come from animals and birds that have been killed in the prescribed way which ensures that no pain whatsoever is inflicted. It is important not to mix meat and milk foods at the same meal. When preparing such foods there must be separate sets of dishes and utensils, one for meat foods and one for milk foods, and these must be washed in separate sinks in the kitchen.

The Mezuzah

The mezuzah is a small parchment scroll on which is written the first two paragraphs of the Shema. The scroll is placed in a small metal case which is then fastened to the doorpost of the front door (in some Jewish homes a case is fastened on the posts of all inside doors). Jews do this because the Shema instructs them to put God's Laws 'upon the doorpost of your house and upon your gates'. Whenever the family passes through the door they touch the mezuzah and this reminds them of God's presence in their home, and of their responsibility to follow God's Law in the life of their home.

A Mezuzah

7 Jewish Holy Books

The Jewish Bible consists of three parts: the Torah (which also contains the Talmud), the Prophets and the Writings.

The Torah

The most important part is the Torah, a title which means 'teaching'. It consists of the five law books of Moses (the Pentateuch), which are Genesis, Exodus, Leviticus, Deuteronomy and Numbers. The Torah is central to the faith of the Jews since it shows them how God works both in creation and history, how they should live in relationship with God, and how they should behave towards their fellow men. The book tells of the Covenant made at Mount Sinai between God and His people, and lists the laws they must keep, the most important of which are the Ten Commandments.

The Torah is always very carefully written by hand on a scroll of parchment, using special ink and a goose quill. Once a Torah is too worn for further use it has to be ceremoniously buried.

The Talmud

This is a more detailed explanation of the law as written in the Torah. At first the Talmud was not written down, but was passed from father to son by word of mouth. The Torah Law needed further explanation since it did not always cover all situations in daily life and, over the centuries, there grew up a vast collection of detailed interpretation. This was put together into a law code called the Mishnah in the 2nd century. Three centuries later the Mishnah and further explanations of the law were put into one large book called the Talmud. There are many volumes which cover many aspects of Jewish life and thought including laws about agriculture, festivals, marriage and divorce, civil and criminal laws, laws concerning the offering of sacrifices, and the laws of purity especially concerning food and drink. All these laws are recorded in the Torah, but the Talmud explains them in much greater detail.

The Prophets

The second part of the Jewish Scriptures is the Prophets which are divided into two sections, the Early Prophets and the Later Prophets. The Early Prophets are an account of the history of the Jews from the time of Joshua up to the capture of Jerusalem by the Babylonians, and the books included in this section are Joshua, Judges, Samuel and Kings. The remainder of the book consists of the prophecies of Isaiah, Jeremiah and Ezekiel. They were men particularly gifted with remarkable powers of insight and their teachings give much guidance for dealing with modern problems. The Later Prophets also include a collection of the teachings of the Twelve Minor Prophets: Amos, Hosea, Micah, etc.

The Writings

This is the final part of the Jewish Bible and it includes a variety of books. The Psalms (many of which are in the Prayer Book), along with Proverbs, the Song of Solomon and Job, contain much poetry. There are books detailing further Jewish history, e.g. Chronicles, Ezra and Nehemiah and other literature, e.g. more poetry in Lamentations, stories in Ruth, Esther and Daniel, and the book of Ecclesiastes which contains the thoughts of a writer who reflects on the mystery of God and on Man's place in His Creation.

Jewish Holy Books in Worship

As all these books, especially the Torah, are very important in the Jewish faith, they have a central place both in public worship in the synagogue and in private prayer. The reading of the Torah is the most important part of the service in the synagogue on the Sabbath. Portions of the Torah are recited weekly so that the whole of the Five Books are read through completely each year.

8 Jewish Beliefs

The Shema

The Jews did not have a written statement of their beliefs for many centuries. The main beliefs are recorded in a prayer called the Shema which is found in the Torah. The principal belief is the unity of God, i.e. there is only one God. Jews say that God is the Creator of Heaven and Earth; He is eternal, ever present, and knows all things. In other words, as He is not part of creation, He is not confined to one place and one time. Furthermore Jews say that no image or picture can ever represent God adequately. Since God makes himself known to men and guides them, He plays an important part in human history.

The Shema was first given to the Jewish people by Moses after God had given him the Ten Commandments on Mount Sinai. The Shema begins with these famous words, 'Hear, O Israel, the Lord our God is one Lord; and you shall love the Lord your God with all your heart, and with all your soul, and with all your might' (Deuteronomy 6:4–5).

--- **The Shema** ---

Hear, O Israel: The Lord our God is one Lord: and thou shalt love the Lord thy God with all thine heart, and with all thy might. And these words, which I command thee this day, shall be in thine heart: and thou shalt teach them diligently unto thy children, and shalt talk of them when thou walkest by the way, and when thou liest down, and when thou risest up. And thou shalt bind them for a sign upon thine hand, and they shall be as frontlets between thine eyes. And thou shalt write them upon the posts of thy house and on thy gates.

The Shema

'Love towards your fellow men'

From the Jewish belief in the unity of God comes the idea of the unity of mankind and the brotherhood of all men. This is expressed clearly in a passage from the Torah, found in the Book of Leviticus, where it says 'Thou shalt love thy neighbour as thyself'. Many Jewish teachings which show how Jews should live a good life have been developed from this belief.

The Ten Commandments

The Jews believe that God revealed Himself to Moses on Mount Sinai to renew the Covenant and to present to His people the teachings outlined in the Ten Commandments. These laws explain more about Jewish beliefs, but they are mainly rules of conduct by which people are expected to live. The Commandments are:

1 I am the Lord Your God; you shall have no other gods before Me.
2 You shall not make any images or idols.
3 You must respect God's name.
4 Remember the Sabbath Day to keep it holy.
5 Honour your father and mother.
6 You shall not commit murder.
7 You shall not commit adultery.
8 You shall not steal.
9 You shall not accuse anyone falsely.
10 You shall not covet (i.e. want something that belongs to another person).

Revelation

Another important Jewish belief is that God has made known His will to His people by revealing Himself to Abraham, Isaac and Jacob, and particularly to Moses. God's will is recorded in the Torah where the greatest revelation of all, the Ten Commandments, are recorded. This process of revelation continued in the teachings of the Prophets.

The Ten Commandments, carved in solid granite on Buckland Beacon, Devon

A famous example of this is seen in the prophecy of Micah when he said, in answer to a question about what God wants men to do, 'Be just, love mercy and walk humbly with God'.

There are three further ideas which are very important in Jewish beliefs. These concern the coming of the Messiah, the Resurrection of the Dead, and Life after Death.

The Coming of the Messiah

Jews say that some time in the future the Messianic Age (from Messiah) will be established. This is a time when God's rule will be set up on earth, the world will be perfect and all mankind will acknowledge God's power and might. There will be no more war, all injustice will cease and righteousness will prevail. This age will be brought into being by the Messiah who is God's messenger. He will be a human being bearing good tidings, and he will have all the qualities of a perfect man.

The Resurrection of the Dead

A belief in the resurrection of the dead has long been held by the Jews. According to the teachings of the Rabbis, the prophet Elijah will help to bring this resurrection into being, and he will announce the coming of the Messiah. Only God knows the time of resurrection since He chooses when it will take place. Jews also say that this idea of resurrection means that when people die their souls will live for ever.

Life after Death

The third belief accepted by Jews is that this present existence is a preparation for living with God after man's earthly life has ended. Following death, man's soul returns to God to live in His presence forever.

The Thirteen Principles of the Faith

In the 12th century Moses Maimonides, a Jewish writer and philosopher, drew up a list of thirteen beliefs which Jews are expected to accept. Although not all Jewish thinkers agreed with Maimonides, the list does give a good idea of what Jews believe. These beliefs explain in more detail the nature of God, the authority of the Law, the teachings of the Prophets, the Coming of the Messiah and the Ressurection of the Dead. The whole statement is printed in the Jewish Prayer Book.

9 Pilgrimage

Jews are not obliged by the rules of their faith to go on pilgrimage. However for many centuries they have visited Jerusalem, their holy city and centre of their religion.

Jerusalem

Ever since the time of King David, i.e. the 10th century BC, Jews have regarded Jerusalem as their holy city since it contained their most important building, the Temple. In all there have been three Temples; the first was built by King Solomon in about 950 BC, and eventually destroyed by the Babylonians in 586 BC. The Second Temple was erected between 520 BC and 516 BC through the efforts of Zerubbabel, the Jewish Governor of Jerusalem. At this time the Jews were ruled by the Persians. This temple survived until the reign of King Herod the Great, who decided to build a much more magnificent temple in its place. This was constructed during the years 19 BC to 9 BC, and it was known as Herod's Temple. Eventually it was destroyed by the Romans in AD 70 after the Jews had rebelled against their conquerors.

When these temples existed, Jews visited them regularly to offer sacrifices to God and to take part in the ceremonies at festival time, e.g. Passover, Pentecost, Tabernacles and New Year. Today all that remains of the Temple is part of the foundations. This is called the 'Western Wall' although some people refer to it as the 'Wailing Wall' because some pilgrims visiting it are overcome by grief on seeing the only remaining part of their great Temple. Many Jews go there to pray every day, and they also think particularly of the difficult and sad times in their history. Some Jews even kiss the stones in the Wall during their devotions.

After the Temple was destroyed the Jews were not allowed to visit its remains. For many centuries the remains were under the control of the Muslims who would not allow the Jews to visit the Wall except once a year on the anniversary of the destruction of the Temple. Their pilgrimage was therefore a sad occasion when they thought about the loss of their most holy place and their own homeland, and prayed for their recovery. However, in 1967, during the war with the Arabs, the situation changed when the Israeli army recaptured Old Jerusalem where the remains of the Temple are found. Ever since that time Jews have been able to visit the Wall whenever they wish.

'Yad Vashen'

While in Jerusalem many Jews visit 'Yad Vashen', the 'eternal memorial', which commemorates all those Jews who died in the Second World War. The main part of the memorial is a large room, which is lit by a single lighted candle. On the floor are written all the names of those who died in concentration camps and any gentiles (non-Jews) who helped them. Many Jews find it a moving experience to visit the memorial, especially if they read the name of a relative or friend amongst those inscribed on the floor.

During the Second World War the Nazis in Germany wanted to keep their race pure. To do this they believed they had to get rid of the Jews and this was done by sending mil-

The Western Wall

lions to concentration camps where many died in gas chambers. This was a dreadful period in Jewish history and is known as the holocaust.

Masada

During the Jewish revolt against the Romans in AD 69 to AD 73, a group of fanatical Jews took refuge in a mountain fortress called Masada in the Judean Desert. Eventually the Romans captured the fortress, but only after the defenders had committed suicide rather than be captured. After the Second World War the site of the fortress was excavated by Israeli archaeologists and it has become an important tourist centre. However many visit it as pilgrims as they remember the commitment of the Masada martyrs who fought so hard to defend their faith and heritage.

10 Jewish Festivals

Throughout the Jewish year, which begins in the autumn, there are a number of important festival occasions. As in many cultures the Jews celebrate the beginning of the New Year. There are also festivals associated with the ancient harvest times of Biblical Palestine. These are Passover, Pentecost, and Tabernacles during which great events in Jewish history are remembered. The other main festivals are Chanukkah and Purim, again celebrating important occasions in history.

The New Year

The Jews work out their calendar according to the phases of the moon. However, in order to keep it in agreement with the Gregorian calendar, extra days are added in some years, thus making them leap years. This means that the Jewish New Year may begin in either September or October. The first day of the New Year is called Rosh Hashanah.

On the evening before, the people attend the synagogue for worship, and then return home to eat a festive meal. This includes apples dipped in honey to symbolize the hope that the New Year will be sweet and pleasant. It is a time for greeting relatives and friends with the wish that they will have a good New Year.

The ten days between Rosh Hashanah and Yom Kippur (the last day of New Year) are called 'the Solemn Days' or 'the Ten Days of Repentance'. Rosh Hashanah is treated as a Sabbath, and on this day Jews remember God's act of creation. On the morning of New Year's Day everyone gathers in the synagogue for a service during which the Shofar horn is blown one hundred times. This is a call to the people from God, the King of the Universe, who is giving them a chance to return to him in repentance, to mend their ways and to be forgiven. The next ten days are a time of 'soul searching': Jews aim to make up for any wrong-doing, so that by Yom Kippur they have made peace with the world, after which they can concentrate on making peace with God.

Yom Kippur (meaning 'the Day of Atonement') is the holiest day in the Jewish Year. 'Atonement' means 'at one', thus for Jews it is a day of trying to be at one with God. It is a day of fasting; as far as possible nothing is eaten or drunk for twenty-five hours. The fast begins one hour before sunset on the eve of Yom Kippur and ends at sunset the next day. Only sick people and those under the age of thirteen are excused. It is not a day of gloom, but rather a time of experiencing God's kindness and His love. The whole day is devoted to prayers and worship in the synagogue. As it is a festive occasion the interior of the synagogue is decorated with white cloths; the ark and the bimah in particular are covered. Everyone, including the Rabbi and other officials, wears white robes as a sign of purity and of the certainty of God's forgiveness.

The prayers on the eve of the fast begin with a prayer known as Kol Nidre (meaning 'all vows'). In this, God is asked to forgive people who have not kept, through forgetfulness or mistake, the promises which they had made to Him. The prayers continue until after midnight. Some adults stay in the synagogue until the early hours of the morning.

Yom Kippur itself is a day of continuous prayers, which include the themes of repentance (returning to God), and charity (showing loving kindness to other people), and the making of solemn promises by the people to improve their daily living. The morning service begins with the Cantor entering the synagogue wearing his white robes. He repeats a prayer which the High Priest recited when he entered the Holy of Holies, the innermost room of the Temple in Jerusalem. Everyone prostrates (kneels bent over with their forehead touching the ground) on the floor of the synagogue as the Cantor solemnly confesses his own sins and the sins of all the people. Passages from the scrolls are read, especially from Leviticus, Numbers and the Prophecy of Isaiah. The passage from Leviticus describes the ritual of the Scapegoat which was held in the Temple (Leviticus 16:20–22). The High Priest placed his hands on the head of a goat while reciting the sins of the people. The goat was then driven into the desert and out of the country; thus the sins of the people were symbolically destroyed.

In the afternoon there is a reading of the Book of Jonah. This continues the theme of repentance and illustrates the universal message of atonement. In the book Jonah proclaimed that the great city of Ninevah was in great danger because of its wickedness. The king and his people fasted and prayed to God who then spared them because of their sincere repentance. In the same way Jews say God will forgive those who are really sorry for any wrongdoing.

The evening service, beginning at sunset, is called Neilah (this means 'closing of the gates'). It recalls the closing of the Temple gates at sunset centuries ago. Up to this point in the festival, the expression 'Inscribe us in the Book of Life' is used in prayer; but it is now changed and the people stand and pray, 'Seal us in the Book of Life'.

The ark remains open throughout the service. Many prayers are spoken, all with the same message that God will forgive anyone who really repents, e.g. 'O grant that we may enter thy gates, we pray thee . . . Have mercy upon us'. The service ends with the congregation repeating the Shema. Finally the Cantor repeats the famous prayer spoken by the prophet Elijah on Mount Carmel when he challenged the people to return and follow the true God. He says, 'Hear, O Israel, the Lord our God, the Lord is One', and the people cry in reply, 'The Lord; He is God', seven times. Last of all, the Shofar horn is sounded. This is a challenge to the people to try to remain 'at one' with God throughout the coming year.

The Festival of Tabernacles

This festival is also called Succoth. It takes place in September or October five days after Yom Kippur and lasts for a week. Taber-

A Jewish family celebrating Succoth at home

nacles recalls the ancient grape and fruit harvest of Israel, but it is also linked with the exodus of the Children of Israel from Egypt. It is said that the Children of Israel made themselves rough shelters or tabernacles when they were in the desert. The main purpose of the festival is to thank God for delivering the people from slavery in Egypt.

Nowadays the people build tabernacles in their gardens, or on the flat roofs of their houses, from branches. The shelters are decorated with citrus fruits (called ethrog) and vegetables, and their roofs are made from woven branches of palm, myrtle and willow. These represent the lulav, which is used in the synagogue services. For the duration of the festival the people live in these shelters, just as their ancestors did when in the desert.

During the services in the synagogue the people hold in their right hands a lulav. This consists of branches of palm bound together with clusters of flowering myrtle and willow. In their left hand they carry some of the ethrog fruits. Each of these has a symbolic meaning. The palm branches stand for uprightness, the willow for humility, the myrtle for faithfulness and the ethrog for affection, simplicity and gentleness. Overall the four plants together represent the peoples of the world living in brotherhood and peace.

The services in the synagogue during Tabernacles are very joyful. They include the reciting by all the congregation of the Hallel (these are hymns of praise, i.e. Psalms 113–118), the waving of the lulav in every direction which shows God's care for the whole world, and of the ethrog showing that God provides all men with food. During the service everyone processes round the synagogue with the lulav and the ethrog, recalling the time when in days past the priests marched round the Temple in Jerusalem carrying palm branches and singing hymns of praise.

The seventh day of the festival is known as Hoshaana Rabba; it is one of the holiest days in the Jewish New Year. Much of the previous night is spent reading the Jewish scriptures. Special prayers are said in the synagogue. Many of these begin with the Hoshaana, the prayer of salvation, i.e. 'Save, we beseech thee'. Seven processions are held; once again the people carry the lulav and the ethrog. The eighth day is called the Day of Assembly, and a special prayer is offered to God by the people for rain and a good harvest, just as their forefathers did in Israel.

Simchat Torah (i.e. 'the Rejoicing of the Law') is the last day of Tabernacles. It is a special time for children. They march in procession in the synagogue carrying candles and banners, and singing hymns, following behind those who carry the scrolls from the ark. The last section of the Torah in Deuteronomy is read by a member of the congregation who is known as 'The Bridegroom of the Law'. Children, even the youngest, are called to the public reading of the Law on this occasion. It reminds Jews that over the centuries such reading of the Law has never ceased, and that the Law is their most priceless possession. Children particularly enjoy this day when they receive presents of sweets and fruit from their parents and friends.

Chanukkah

For eight days in November and December Chanukkah or the Festival of Dedication (or of Lights) is held. The festival commemorates the courage of a small band of Jews, led by Judas Maccabaeus, the son of a priest, who fought to preserve their faith against Antiochus of Syria. Two thousand years ago Antiochus ruled the Jews and he tried to force his own pagan religion on them. He forbade the Jews to observe the Sabbath, he destroyed the scrolls of the Torah, and desecrated the Temple by putting pagan idols inside it and ordering the Jews to worship them. Many refused and as a result were executed. Judas led a revolt against Antiochus and after three years of struggle the Syrians were defeated. Judas then set about purifying the Temple. The menorah (temple lamps) were lit, but it was discovered that there was only enough oil to last for one day. However, miraculously, it lasted eight days and Judas proclaimed the festival of Chanukkah to commemorate the event.

During the celebration both at home and in the synagogue eight candles in a special menorah are lit. On the first night one candle is lit, followed each evening by an additional candle until on the eighth evening all are burning. Whenever a candle is lit a blessing is said. During the daily prayers Psalms 113–118 are recited and a special prayer is added to the Amidah. This outlines the events of Chanukkah two thousand years ago, and gives thanks to God for the miracles which occurred and for the deliverance from the pagan king.

Parties and pageants telling stories of the Maccabean heroes are organized for the children. They play games with a four-sided spinning top: on its sides are written the first letters of four Hebrew words which mean 'a great miracle happened here'. In Israel today there are many Chanukkah events, including a torchlight procession along the road from Modin, where Judas began the revolt, to Mount Zion, the site of the Temple in Jerusalem.

Purim

In early spring, in February or March, the Festival of Purim is held. 'Purim' means 'lots' and this name is used because, over two thousand years ago, Haman, the chief minister of the Persian king, cast lots in order to work out the best day for putting into operation his plan to destroy all the Jews living in Persia. The whole story is written in the Book of Esther, which is read aloud during the evening and morning services on Purim.

The story begins with Haman vowing to exterminate all the Jews in Persia because Mordecai, a Jew, has refused to bow down before him. On the day indicated by the lots Haman went to the Persian king, Ahasuerus. He told him many lies about the Jews, and he offered the king a large fortune if he would order the execution of all the Jews. The king agreed and sent a proclama-tion throughout the country saying that all Jews should be slaughtered on a certain day. Mordecai heard of the plot and he informed his cousin, Esther, who was Queen of Persia. Esther decided that she must help her fellow Jews, but she could only do that by speaking of the plot with her husband. This would put her life in danger since normally she only went into the king's presence when summoned. Therefore she asked Mordecai and all the Jews to join her in a fast for three days when she would seek God's help in that difficult time.

After her fast Esther went to the king hoping to gain an audience. This was granted, and Esther invited both the king and Haman to a banquet. Haman was delighted since it was an honour to dine with the king and his queen. Haman then had a gallows built on which he planned to hang Mordecai before the banquet so that he could enjoy the feasting all the more. During the night before the banquet Ahasuerus learned how Mordecai had once saved his life, and to show his gratitude he ordered Haman to dress Mordecai in royal robes, and then arrange for him to ride through the city streets as a reward for his loyalty. At the banquet Esther denounced Haman for plotting against the Jews. The king was so angry that he ordered Haman to be hanged on the gallows he had built for Mordecai. The king then agreed to cancel his proclamation; thus through the efforts of Esther the lives of all the Jews in Persia were saved.

Nowadays the day before Purim is kept as a fast in memory of Esther's three-day fast. During the reading of the Book of Esther, whenever the name of Haman is mentioned the people hiss and stamp their feet; the children noisily wave football-type rattles called graggers to drown the sound of the traitor's name. Purim is a time of rejoicing; the children perform plays which narrate the events, and everyone goes to parties. A special cake is eaten called Hamantaschen. This is a three-cornered pastry filled with poppy seeds. In Israel the story of Esther is retold in carnivals and processions held in the streets of the main cities.

Passover

Passover or Pesach is the most important of the Jewish festivals. It is celebrated in springtime in March or April. During Biblical times the festival was associated with the barley harvest in Israel, but nowadays it is a celebration of the liberation of the Children of Israel from slavery in Egypt. The name 'Passover' which is often used for this festival recalls the last plague sent upon the Egyptians by God. Moses said God would send the Angel of Death to 'pass over' the land of Egypt to slay all the Egyptian first-born sons. Moses instructed the Children of Israel to mark their doorposts with the blood of a newly-sacrificed lamb so that their children would not be affected by the Angel.

The festival is also called the Feast of Unleavened Bread. It is said that the Children of Israel, in their anxiety to leave Egypt, only had time to make thin flat cakes of bread. As they did not use any yeast it was called unleavened bread. Because of this a Jewish home must be thoroughly cleaned before Passover, and all food containing leaven, i.e. yeast, must be removed from the house. Some pieces of bread are actually hidden by the mother and the children enjoy looking for them, especially as the finders receive a prize. The special Passover crockery and utensils are also brought out for the duration of the festival. It is the only time in the year when they are used, the everyday crockery and utensils are put on one side.

The Seder plate

There are special services in the synagogue when, apart from the usual prayers, there are readings from the Scriptures describing the events. However, the main celebration of the festival takes place in the home; this is the Seder Service which vividly illustrates the story and meaning of Passover. 'Seder' means 'order' and it indicates that, wherever Jewish families meet in the world, they follow the same order of service.

The service takes place at the table around which the family sits to eat a specially prepared meal. The table is covered with a fine cloth on which the best crockery is laid along with a wine glass for each person, and silver candlesticks, if the family possesses them. Each person also has a Haggadah which is a book containing the Passover story. The Seder plate is placed in the centre of the table; on this are special foods, each one having a symbolic meaning. There are:

Three matzoth, which are thin wafers of unleavened bread and a reminder of the bread the Children of Israel took with them when they left Egypt.

A roasted shank bone representing the Passover Lamb.

A roasted egg; a symbol of new life and resurrection; it has new life within it although on the outside it appears dead; it is also a reminder of spring.

Sprigs of parsley; to be dipped in salt water to remind the Jews of the tears of the slaves and of the salt sea.

Bitter herbs; a reminder of the bitterness of slavery.

Haroset: a mixture of apple, nuts, wine and cinnamon, which looks like mortar and represents the hard labour of the slaves in Egypt.

Besides this, there is on the table a dish of salt water, and an extra wine glass. The extra glass is known as Elijah's cup and the door is left ajar for Elijah. This reminds Jews of their belief that one day Elijah will return, announcing the beginning of the age of the Messiah when all mankind will be redeemed and God's kingdom will be established on earth in justice and peace.

The service begins with the Kiddush ceremony. Four glasses of wine are drunk during the service. These remind the Jews of the four ways by which God promised Moses He would redeem the Children of Israel. The father then washes his hands, dips the parsley in the salt water and passes a piece to each person. In front of the father is a plate on which are three matzoth. He takes the middle matzoth and says, 'This is the bread of affliction that our fathers ate in the land of Egypt. Let all who are hungry come and eat. Let all who are in want come and celebrate the Passover with us'. It is then broken in half: one piece is eaten during the meal and the remainder at the end of the meal.

The youngest member of the family then asks four questions:

Why is this night different from other nights?
Why on this night do we eat only bitter herbs?
Why on this night do we dip our herbs?
Why on this night do we all recline as we eat?

Everyone joins in the reply, 'We were slaves under Pharaoh in Egypt and the Lord Our God brought us out with a mighty hand' (Deuteronomy 6:21). Then the story of the deliverance of the slaves from bondage is read from the Haggadah. At intervals wine is drunk and hymns of praise are sung. This part of the service closes with everyone reciting together the solemn words, 'In every generation it is man's duty to regard himself as if he had gone forth from Egypt'. More wine is drunk, followed by the repetition of words of praise and thanksgiving to God, and the singing of psalms, e.g. 113 and 114, which fit the occasion.

The second cup of wine is blessed and after further blessings, pieces from two of the matzoth are passed to each person. Next

The Passover meal

the bitter herb is dipped in the haroset. More of the matzoth are broken, and the real meal begins. During this each person eats a piece of matzoth like a sandwich with the bitter herb inside it. At the end of the meal everyone is given, for dessert, a piece of the matzoth broken at the beginning of the meal. Grace is spoken together and a third cup of wine is drunk.

Then the second part of the Seder Service commences; this includes poems, hymns and songs about the Passover, and about the way God saved the Children of Israel from slavery. Finally everyone drinks the fourth cup of wine, and the service is concluded. In this way, the Jews relive the great events of Passover and once again they are reminded of this great struggle for freedom, and how it is still relevant in the world today.

Pentecost

Fifty days after Passover, in May or June, the Feast of Pentecost or Shavout is celebrated. It is also called the Feast of Weeks because it was held seven weeks after Passover and commemorates the giving of the Ten Commandments to Moses at Mount Sinai. It used to be associated with the harvests of Israel when in the past the people brought to the Temple baskets of the first crops of barley, wheat and fruit. Today synagogues are decorated with flowers and plants; this is a way of thanking God for his kindness to men.

For most of the first night of the festival many Jews sit up in the synagogue and read from the Torah and the Talmud. This preparation is a reminder of God's command to the Children of Israel when they were in the desert; that no one should approach the borders of Mount Sinai for three days before the giving of the Ten Commandments. The morning service in the synagogue includes the reading of that part of the Torah which describes the giving of the Commandments; during this reading all the members of the congregation stand. The two tablets above the ark in the synagogue on which are written the first words of the Commandments, are a constant reminder of this event at Mount Sinai.

The Book of Ruth is read during the Festival. The description of Ruth's acceptance of the Jewish faith is particularly important. The book also gives a clear account of harvest-time in ancient Israel, and underlines the Jewish duty to take care of those in need, since it shows how the poor and needy were allowed to glean any corn that was left over by the harvesters. Furthermore, the people are reminded that King David was descended from Ruth, and that he died during this festival.

In the home a festival meal is eaten after morning service. On the table are two round loaves decorated with a ladder which are a reminder of Moses' ascent up Mount Sinai to receive the Ten Commandments from God.

The Fast of the Ninth Ab

This fast day commemorates the destruction of the First Temple (built by King Solomon in Jerusalem) by the Babylonians in 586 BC and the destruction of Herod's Temple by the Romans in AD 70. The fast takes place in the late summer, and involves the reading of some suitable passages from the Scriptures (e.g. from Exodus, Isaiah and Jeremiah) during the morning and afternoon services in the synagogue. The Book of Lamentations is also read. This is very appropriate since it describes the destruction of Jerusalem and the capture of Judea by the Babylonians, and the severe suffering of the Jewish people. While listening to the reading, the people sit on low stools and benches, or even on the floor, with their heads bowed as if in mourning.

There is also a custom of going to the cemetery on Ninth Ab to visit the family graves. This has nothing to do with the destruction of the Temple, but it is linked with the ancient custom of visiting cemeteries on all fast days.

·Glossary·

Alenu	closing prayer used in Sabbath Day worship (cf. page 37)
Amidah	prayer offered silently by Jews in the synagogue as they face the ark (cf. page 37)
Ark	large cupboard in the synagogue containing the scrolls of the Law (cf. page 30)
Bar-mitzvah	ceremony in the synagogue when a Jewish boy religiously becomes an adult (cf. page 34)
Bat-mitzvah	similar ceremony to bar-mitzvah but for girls (cf. page 35)
Bimah	platform in the synagogue from which the scrolls are read (cf. page 31)
Canaan	old name for Israel or Palestine; used in the time of the early Jews (cf. page 27)
Cantor	singer trained to lead worship in the synagogue (cf. page 33)
Chanukkah	festival held in November and December (cf. page 45)
Circumcision	ceremony held eight days after the birth of a baby boy (cf. page 34)
Covenant	agreement made between God and His people (cf. page 27)
Ethrog	citrus fruit used in ceremonies during the Feast of Tabernacles (cf. page 45)
Haggadah	service book used during celebration of the Feast of Passover (cf. page 47)
Haroset	mixture of apple, nuts, wine and cinnamon eaten at the Seder meal during Passover (cf. page 47)
Havdalah	prayer spoken at home to mark the close of the Sabbath (cf. page 32)
Holocaust	suffering of the Jews during the Second World War when millions were put to death by the Nazis (cf. page 43)
Hoshaana Rabba	seventh day of the Feast of Tabernacles (cf. page 45)
Jerusalem	holy city of the Jews in Israel (cf. page 41)
Kaddish	prayer of sanctification used in synagogue worship (cf. page 37)
Ketubah	marriage contract signed by the bridegroom (cf. page 36)
Kiddhushin	Jewish wedding ceremony (cf. page 35)
Kiddush	ceremony held in the home at the beginning of the Sabbath (cf. page 32)
Kol Nidre	prayer with which ceremonies begin in the synagogue on the eve of Yom Kippur (cf. page 43)
Kosher	food prepared according to the Jewish Law (cf. page 37)
Lulav	branches of palm bound with willow and myrtle used at Feast of Tabernacles (cf. page 45)
Manna	'bread from heaven' given to the Children of Israel while they journeyed through the desert to Canaan (cf. page 32)
Matzoth	unleavened bread eaten at Passover (cf. page 47)
Menorah	seven-branched candlestick used in the synagogue (cf. page 31)

Mezuzah	small box containing a piece of scroll which is fastened to the doorpost of a Jewish home (cf. page 38)
Minyan	group of ten males required to assemble together before worship can take place (cf. page 33)
Mishnah	collection of Jewish teaching written down in the 2nd century AD interpreting the Torah (cf. page 38)
Neilah	evening service held in the synagogue at Yom Kippur (cf. page 44)
Ninth Ab	fast day commemorating the destruction of the Temple in Jerusalem (cf. page 49)
Passover	spring festival celebrating the deliverance of the Children of Israel from slavery in Egypt by Moses (cf. page 47)
Pentecost	festival held in May or June commemorating the giving of the Ten Commandments to Moses (cf. page 49)
Phylacteries	small leather boxes fastened by Jewish men to the forehead and forearm during worship (cf. page 32)
Purim	festival held in February or March to remember the saving of the Jews from destruction by the Persians (cf. page 46)
Rabbi	leader of the local Jewish Community (cf. page 33)
Rosh Hashanah	first day of the Jewish New Year (cf. page 43)
Sabbath	Jewish holy day; lasts from Friday sunset to Saturday sunset (cf. page 31)
Seder	name of the service followed by Jewish families when celebrating the Passover at home (cf. page 47)
Shofar	ram's horn blown in Jewish worship (cf. page 43)
Siddur	Jewish prayer book (cf. page 37)
Simchat Torah	last day of the Feast of Tabernacles (cf. page 45)
Succoth	alternative name for the Feast of Tabernacles (cf. page 44)
Synagogue	Jewish place of worship; means 'place or house of assembly' (cf. page 30)
Tabernacles	festival held in September or October; linked with harvest-time and the journeying of the Children of Israel in the desert (cf. page 44)
Tallith	prayer shawl worn by Jewish men (cf. page 32)
Talmud	Jewish holy writings which give a detailed explanation of the Jewish Law (cf. page 38)
Tefillin	alternative name for **Phylacteries**
Torah	Jewish holy writings; consists of the five Law Books of Moses (cf. page 38)
Western Wall	sole remains of the Temple in Jerusalem, much visited by Jews (cf. page 41)
Yad Vashen	memorial set up in Jerusalem to commemorate the Jews who died in the holocaust during the Second World War (cf. page 42)
Yarmulka	skull cap worn by Jewish men (cf. page 32)
Yom Kippur	last day of the New Year celebrations; the holiest day in the Jewish year (cf. page 43)

Activities

1 Important Things to Remember and Understand

Special words and ideas: bar-mitzvah; circumcision; covenant; holocaust; kosher; menorah; Passover; rabbi; Sabbath; synagogue; tallith; tefillin; Torah.

2 Important Things to Find Out

Find out what it is like inside a synagogue; if there is a synagogue in the area ask the Rabbi to give you a conducted tour.
Ask a Jewish boy to tell you about his bar-mitzvah ceremony.

3 Important Things to Discuss

Jews have constantly suffered persecution. What reasons can you suggest for this?
Some people believe it was wrong for the modern state of Israel to be established because it has caused too much trouble in the Middle East. What do you think?
It seems that very few Jewish young people get into trouble with the law. Can you suggest why this is so?

4 Important Things to Do

Find out if it is possible to visit a Jewish home around Passover-time to discover what this festival means to Jews.
Ask a Jewish housewife to come and talk about her life at home.

5 Written Work

a What contribution did Abraham and Moses make in estabishing the Jewish faith?
b In what ways do Jewish people worship God both at home and in the synagogue?
c Explain the many ways in which Jewish religious laws affect everyday life for Jewish people.

CHAPTER 3

·Islam·

1 What is Islam?

Islam is the second largest religion in the world after Christianity. If you look back to the map at the front of the book you will see the principal areas it covers. It did not really have a founder but developed as a separate religion distinct from Judaism and Christianity. The revelation from God was given to the people through the prophet Muhammad who lived in Arabia from AD 570 to AD 632 so he is very highly respected. He be-lieved that he had been chosen by Allah (the Arabic word for 'God') to take his message to the people. The word 'Islam' means 'submission to Allah', and the name given to a person who has submitted or surrendered his life to Allah is 'Muslim'. The star and crescent of the moon is their symbol: the star to guide and the moon to light the way as in hot desert countries. In the same way Islam guides men on the journey through life.

2 Arabia at the Time of Muhammad

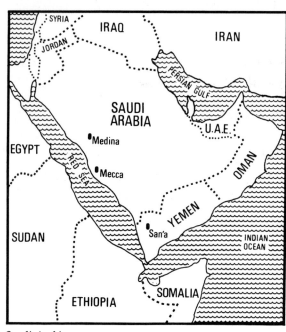

Saudi Arabia

Most of Arabia consists of a high plateau of sandy wastes including the two largest sand deserts in the world with a mountain barrier virtually shutting off the interior from the sea on three sides. There are few passes and very little lowland on the Red Sea coast but more on the east side around the Persian Gulf. Settlements sprang up mainly at oases, or watering holes, where nomads grazed their animals, or along the sea coasts. The difficulty of the land and the extremely dry hot climate made farming difficult apart from growing things like date palms and citrus fruits around the oases but one asset the nomadic tribes had was the camel. Initially using it for war and raids on other tribes, the Bedouin people soon began to use it for transporting goods and a whole series of trade routes was established across Arabia.

Along these routes, caravans of camels

carried cargoes of perfumes, spices, oils and gold from the East to the ports of the Mediterranean coast for shipment. Towns like Medina, Mecca and San'a grew up either at the oases or at crossing points of these routes and many Arabs earned their living by trading. It was like this when Muhammad was born in Mecca.

Religion in Arabia

Originally the Arabs had animistic beliefs which meant that they worshipped the spirits which they believed inhabited such things as stones and trees. Later many adopted polytheistic ideas as a result of which they began to worship many gods. There were also some people who worshipped one God, particularly Jews and Christians. Their forefathers had settled there after being persecuted in their homeland, Judea, during Roman times.

Mecca was the most important religious centre in Arabia, because a temple called the Ka'ba had been built in the city. Muslim tradition says that it had been built by the prophet Abraham when he visited the city with his son, Ishmael. The Ka'ba was revered by all Arabs and, since it was a great centre of pilgrimage, it was visited by many people each year.

3 The Life of Muhammad

His Early Life

Muhammad was born into the Quaraysh tribe in Mecca in AD 570. His father's name was Abdullah, son of Abdul Muttalib, but he died in Yathrib (later Medina) before his son was born, so Muhammad never saw his father. His mother died when he was only six so Muhammad was then left an orphan. He was brought up first by his grandfather, and then by his uncle, Abu Talib, who was a merchant in Mecca.

His Early Years in Mecca

Muhammad accompanied his uncle on trading missions to Syria. In time he became a caravan leader and later was employed by Khadija, a widow and wealthy businesswoman, as her agent. In Mecca Muhammad was greatly respected for his honesty, fairmindedness and reliability.

At this time he helped to solve a problem concerning the Ka'ba. A flood had damaged the temple wall and the holy black stone had been dislodged. While the repair work was in progress, a quarrel had broken out between the tribes about who should have the honour of restoring the stone to its position. Eventually they agreed to ask the first man who came to the Ka'ba the next day to settle the dispute. Muhammad was the first man to arrive and, after hearing about the problem, he spread a cloak on the ground and placed the holy stone on it. He then told the chiefs of the tribes to take hold of a corner of the cloak, and carry the stone to its place together. In this way the honour of replacing the stone was shared. As a result the people of Mecca respected him even more and praised him for his wisdom. Some say it was at this time that he was first called Muhammad (this means 'the praised'). Previously his name had been Kothan.

Khadija, who was now forty years old, saw that, under Muhammad's guidance, her business had become more prosperous. She therefore decided to propose marriage to Muhammad even though he was fifteen years younger than her. Muhammad accepted, and they had a very successful married life together. Khadija bore Muhammad six children, four daughters and two sons, but both the sons died in infancy.

Muhammad's Vision and His Call to Be a Prophet

At this time Muhammad began to spend much time praying and meditating in the desert around Mecca. One night, while in a cave on Mount Hira, an angel appeared to him. The angel, who said he was Gabriel, ordered Muhammad to read a scroll which he was holding. He also announced that henceforth Muhammad was 'the messenger of God'. Muhammad explained that he could not read, so the angel repeated the words three times until Muhammad found that miraculously he could say them by heart. He was then instructed to return to Mecca and preach the message 'There is but one God, Allah'. From that time onwards the angel appeared to Muhammad on many occasions throughout his lifetime.

Muhammad's Preaching in Mecca

At first Muhammad was frightened by the vision and he even thought of committing suicide. However Khadija realized that his vision was genuine and she gave him her full support. When Muhammad began preaching in Mecca the people were very hostile since they were mainly idol-worshippers. The Ka'ba was the centre of worship and much money was made from the pilgrims who regularly visited it. Nevertheless Muhammad persevered.

Some Meccans accepted his message, including Khadija, his cousin Ali, and Zaid, a slave. Also some pilgrims, who had come from Medina, became believers. When they took the message back with them it spread rapidly amongst the people of that city.

Muhammad's Migration to Medina

Following the death of his uncle Abu Talib, who had given him protection, and Khadija in AD 621, Muhammad and his followers suffered increasing persecution from the Meccans. Eventually he moved to Medina in AD 622, where he was given sanctuary by his Medinan followers in the hope that he would be able to control the various warring tribes there. This migration is known as the Hijra by Muslims and it is the date from which they begin their calendar. (Their dates are AH meaning 'after the Hijra' or 'after the migration'.) Slowly Muhammad established himself in the city and became its ruler as many more of its inhabitants be-

A 19th-century lithograph of Medina

came Muslims and accepted his leadership.

Muhammad's Return to Mecca and His Death

Muhammad realized that if Islam was really to take over in Arabia it would need to be accepted in the holy city of Mecca. His great wish now was to return to Mecca and make the Ka'ba the centre of the worship of Allah. His revelations told him that he would need to use force to spread the faith further. There began a series of skirmishes, sometimes won by the Meccans, sometimes by the Muslims. The first and most important of these was at Badr where Muhammad won a victory against considerable odds thus convincing his followers that Allah was truly on his side.

The fighting culminated in AD 630 when the Muslims advanced on Mecca, the city capitulated and nearly all the citizens accepted Islam. Immediately Muhammad purified the Ka'ba by destroying all the idols, then re-dedicated it as a temple for the worship of Allah. Islam continued to spread and by the time Muhammad died two years later in Medina nearly the whole of Arabia was united in accepting Islam.

4 The Spread of Islam

After Muhammad's death the Muslims were led in turn by four of his companions. These were Abu Bakr, Umar, Uthman and Ali. They are known as 'the Rightly-guided Caliphs'. (Caliph comes from an Arab phrase meaning 'successor'.) During the thirty years of their rule Islam spread rapidly to the east, the west and the north of Arabia as Muhammad's followers conducted their 'holy war'. Just as Muhammad had said, they felt that it was right if necessary to spread the faith of Islam by fighting. This advance continued steadily over several centuries especially in Eastern Europe and in the Indian sub-continent.

In the East

Persia was conquered by AD 651, and over the next fifty years the Muslims pushed further eastwards. In AD 713 they moved into North-west India where they invaded the Indus Valley. By AD 1000 they had established a great empire in India with Delhi as its capital. They remained in control in India for many centuries, particularly during the period of the great Mogul Empire. This was established in the 15th century and it continued until the mid-19th century when the last Muslim emperor was deposed by the British.

In the West

By the end of the 7th century the Muslims had subdued all of North Africa, and in AD 714 the conquest of Spain was accomplished. Eventually the Muslim armies were defeated by Charles Martel, the King of the Franks, at the Battle of Tours in AD 732, and any further expansion of Islam in the west was prevented. Over the next four centuries the Muslims were slowly driven out of Spain altogether, but they remained in control in North Africa.

In the North

To the north-west of Arabia the Muslim armies met strong opposition from the Christian Byzantine Empire. Even so, in AD 636, Syria was conquered; thereafter progress was much slower as they moved into Asia Minor. Over the next one hundred years several attempts were made to capture Constantinople, the capital of the Byzantine Empire. It was not until the Turks controlled all of Asia Minor that Islam spread further. In 1453 they captured Constantinople, then slowly moved towards Vienna in Austria which they unsuccessfully attempted to take in 1529. After that their influence slowly declined in Eastern Europe. Nowadays, apart from in Yugoslavia, there are very few Muslims in that area.

5 Islam Today

The message of Islam continued to spread into Africa and the Far East, not by conquest, but by merchants and traders. Nowadays most Muslims live within a broad band stretching across the world eastwards from West Africa to the Islands of Indonesia; within this are such countries as Nigeria, Libya, Somalia, Pakistan, Bangladesh and Malaysia.

Today Muslims are generally divided into two main groups: the Sunnis and the Shi'a (also known as the Shi'ites). They both accept the main beliefs and practices, but there is one important difference, which dates back to the early days of Islam. In AD 661 a quarrel broke out about Muhammad's successor, i.e. the Caliph. A group who are now called Shi'a would only accept a member of Muhammad's family as the true Caliph. This could only mean Ali, the Fourth Rightly-guided Caliph, who was Muhammad's cousin. They claim that only the descendants of Ali are the true leaders of Islam. Nowadays they use the title 'Imam' rather than 'Caliph'. However the Sunnis do not accept this since they have always declared that all the Rightly-guided Caliphs were true successors of Muhammad.

6 Muslim Worship

The Mosque: the Muslim Place of Worship
The building where Muslims worship together is called a mosque. The word 'mosque' means 'place of prayer' or 'place of prostration'. (There are more details about this on page 62.) The mosque is the focal

The Omar Ali Saifuddin Mosque, Brunei

point of a Muslim's devotional life and of the Muslim community. Apart from the main hall where worship is conducted, the mosque has facilities for washing, for study, for teaching children and for preparing the dead for burial.

The Exterior

Most mosques are rectangular in shape and very plain on the outside with little or no decoration. However, some mosques are very fine buildings and magnificent examples of Muslim architecture, e.g. the Sultan Ahmet Mosque in Istanbul.

Mosques can easily be recognized since they have two very distinctive features: minarets and domes. The minaret is a tall, thin tower from the top of which the call to prayer goes out five times each day. This verbal call to prayer is usually made by an official called the muezzin, although in some modern mosques a loudspeaker system is used. Most mosques have an onion-shaped dome symbolizing the universe.

The Interior

The main hall of the mosque is simply furnished. There are no seats, but there may be rugs or carpets on the floor. In one wall there is a recess or niche; this is called the mihrab. It is positioned in the middle of the qibla wall. 'Qibla' is from a word meaning 'direction', as this wall indicates the direction of Mecca, the Muslims' holy city. Muslims must face in this direction when praying. To the right of the mihrab is a small platform or pulpit called the minbar. The walls are often richly decorated with patterns of flowers and geometric designs which are sometimes fashioned from mosaic tiles, and Arabic inscriptions of the name of Allah, Muhammad or quotations from the Qur'an, their holy book. No pictures or statues, especially of people, are allowed as these are forbidden by Islamic law. God alone is to be worshipped.

As Muslims must be clean before they pray there are facilities for washing at the mosque. In many old mosques there may be a fountain in the courtyard or an open-air pool. However, in modern mosques, especially in the West, there are cloakrooms for men and women where they wash and where they leave their shoes as they must worship God barefoot. Some mosques have an area reserved for women which they use when worship takes place. The women are

Inside a mosque in El Hamel, showing the mihrab and minbar

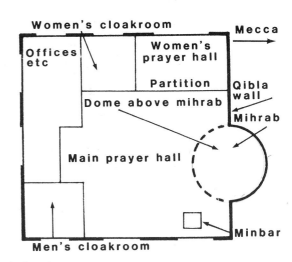

A plan of a mosque

58

separated from the men by a screen; they can hear everything but they cannot be seen. More usually women take their place behind the men in the mosque or remain at home for worship.

The Ka'ba

This is the most famous and probably the most ancient Muslim place of worship. It was built in Mecca, many years before the time of Muhammad to house the 'Black Stone'. Tradition says it was built by Abraham. You will remember that Muhammad is said to have been given his name after solving a problem concerning the Black Stone which had become dislodged from the Ka'ba wall. This Black Stone is kissed and touched by countless numbers of pilgrims seeking forgiveness of their sins.

The Ka'ba is a plain stone building in the shape of a cube eight metres high, situated in the courtyard of the Great Mosque in Mecca. It is covered with a cloth of black brocade on which is embroidered Arabic quotations from the Qur'an in gold. This is called the Kiswa, and it is renewed each year. The building acts as the focal point for Muslims throughout the world.

The Ka'ba

Worship in the Mosque

The Holy Day

There is no particular holy day in Islam as in other religions. However, on Fridays at noon, Muslim men and women meet in the mosque for corporate prayer. Apart from this period of prayer-time, Friday is an ordinary working day for Muslims.

Preparation

Before praying Muslims must wash in the prescribed manner and leave their shoes in the cloakroom or at the door (see page 61).

Worshippers in a Birmingham mosque

The Form of Worship

This act of prayer is led by the Imam or leader of the local Muslim community. He has no special training; he is simply someone whom his fellow Muslims respect and who knows the Qur'an well. The Imam stands at the front facing the mihrab with the people standing in rows behind him. As he goes through the prayer sequence, the people do the same, keeping in time with him. The Imam also preaches a sermon from the minbar. He encourages them to live up to the standards Muhammad laid down, and also by this means he keeps the people in touch with the Islamic attitude to current events. After worship is over they all return to their work. This includes the Imam who is not a paid official. He has an ordinary job like anyone else.

7 Muslim Beliefs and Duties

The main Muslim beliefs are found in the teaching of the Qur'an, the holy book of Islam. These are belief in one God, in His Prophets, His Books including the Qur'an, in the Day of Resurrection, in the Day of Judgment and in Life after Death. There are also Five Pillars or Principles which regulate a Muslim's relationship with God and which guide his daily living. The Five Pillars are: the Creed of Islam, Prayer, Fasting, Almsgiving and Pilgrimage.

The First Pillar: The Creed of Islam

This creed is a statement of belief containing one sentence which roughly translated means: 'There is no god but God, and Muhammad is His Prophet'. This statement is called the Shahada, and it is spoken by Muslims many times each day. They say the words on rising in the morning, throughout each day, before going to bed, and as they are dying.

This belief in one god is the foundation of Islam. To Muslims God is ONE; He is unique. Various names are used for God which help Muslims understand His nature. He is Allah, the All-Powerful, the Creator and Sustainer of the whole world. Thus He is in control of the life and death of all creatures. He is the Sovereign, the Law-Giver, and the Administrator of all in heaven and earth. As He is considered the source of all guidance, He is called the Just, the Forgiving and the Merciful. Since Muslims believe God accompanies them wherever they go, they also call God the All-Knowing, the All-Seeing and the All-Hearing. In all, Muslims have ninety-nine ways of referring to God, which they call the Ninety-nine Beautiful Names.

Muslims must worship only God and give Him their complete loyalty; they must love or fear none more than God. This belief in God fills every part of Muslim life, and it is expressed in many ways. For example before any simple act, Muslims say 'Bismillah' ('in the name of God') and in making plans for the future they say 'Insha Allah' ('God willing'). Such statements are an outward expression of the Muslims' complete surrender of their whole lives to God.

The Prophets

Muslims believe that God revealed His message to men by means of human beings chosen for this purpose; these are the

The Five Pillars

Prophets. Muslims are required to believe in and respect all the Prophets of God from Adam to Jesus. Since they believe Muhammad completed the work of all previous prophets, they believe that prophethood came to an end with him. They say that God made Muhammad the seal of all the prophets and that the total way of life God wished men to follow was completed in Muhammad's teaching. Muhammad is greatly revered by Muslims, but *not* worshipped. He himself forbade this. This was underlined by Muhammad's successor Abu Bakr, who, shortly after Muhammad's death, said 'Let him know whosoever worshipped Muhammad, that Muhammad is dead, but whosoever worshipped God, let him know that God lives and never dies'.

The Second Pillar: Prayer

Muslims are taught that they must pray five times each day, i.e. on rising in the morning, at noon, in mid-afternoon, after sunset and just before retiring to bed. When they pray they must face in the direction of Mecca and follow a special routine. As they pray they believe they are united with other Muslims throughout the world who are praying at the same time wherever they may be.

Reasons for Praying

Muslims are taught that they must pray to praise the divine greatness of God, to seek strength to live good lives and to help them serve their fellow men. By praying they show that they are ready to accept obediently the path set out for them by God, and also they are constantly reminded of God throughout the day.

Types of Prayer

There are two main types in Islam: Du'ah and Salat. Du'ah is not compulsory; it is informal and private prayer, and can be carried out whenever a Muslim chooses. The word 'du'ah' means 'petition'; therefore in Du'ah prayer Muslims seek God's mercy and grace, and ask for His help and guidance. They may also use a string of ninety-nine beads to help them as they praise God. They count the beads as they recite the Ninety-Nine Beautiful Names of God.

Salat is the special pattern of prayer which is performed five times each day. It consists of a series of ritual movements. This prayer is compulsory for all Muslims over the age of ten years. Prayer can be performed alone or in a group, at home, at work or in a mosque. In fact Muslims say that they can pray anywhere since they believe God is in every place.

Preparation for Prayer

Muslims say they must be as clean and as pure as possible before praying. They always carefully wash their faces, ears, eyes, hands, arms up to the elbow, their feet and their legs up to the knee. In a mosque this is done either at a fountain or in a special cloakroom. They must be barefoot during prayer; this is a symbol of their surrender to God and of their humility before Him. They must cover their heads before beginning prayer. The men wear a topi, a small cap; women wear a burka, a shawl, which covers their head and shoulders.

Evening prayers at a mosque in Peshawar

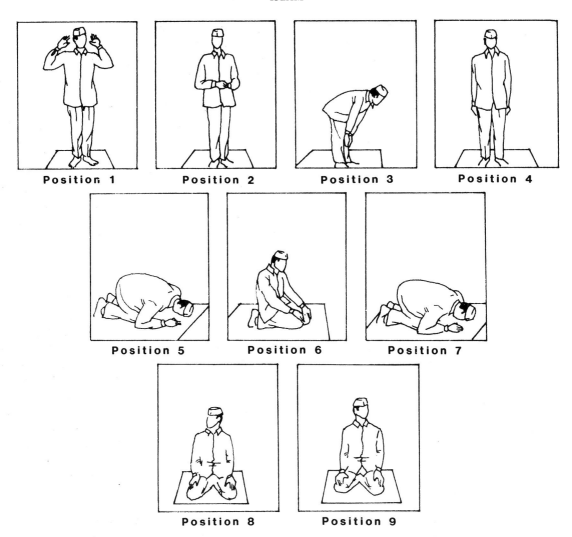

A rak'ah

The Salat Method of Prayer

Often a Muslim will know a time of prayer is approaching, since he may hear the 'Adhan', the call to prayer made by the muezzin. He makes the required preparations, then begins his prayers. First of all a prayer mat is placed on the floor so that he faces Mecca. He begins by repeating the call to prayer, and then carries out a series of movements called a rak'ah. First of all he stands up and lifts his hands to his ears with the palms facing forward. Then he puts his right hand on his left, and places both across his body on his stomach. Next he bows forward, putting his hands on his knees. He stands up straight and then prostrates, that is kneels down and leans forward, placing his forehead on the ground. Next he sits back on his heels, then prostrates once again.

He must go through this sequence of movements several times depending on the time of day. On rising he completes two rak'ahs, just after sunset he carries out three rak'ahs, and on the other three daily occasions of prayers there are four rak'ahs to be done each time. To complete his prayers he sits back on his heels, then turns his head to look over his right shoulder, and finally he looks over his left shoulder. As he does this he says, 'Peace be upon you and God's blessing'. In this way he remembers his fellow Muslims wherever they are.

While performing Salat, set passages and prayers in Arabic which are mostly taken from the Qur'an are repeated. At the end of any prayer-time any personal private prayers may be spoken.

The Third Pillar: Almsgiving

Muslims believe that all they possess has been given to them by God in trust, and it is their duty to give money to charity. The Qur'an says Muslims must give up $2\frac{1}{2}$% of the value of their total wealth each year. It must be used for the poor, for slaves wanting to buy their freedom, for those who are owed money, for travellers and for community projects.

It is not thought of as a tax on wealth. For the whole Muslim community it is a way of redistributing wealth. The word Muslims use for this almsgiving is 'zakat', which means 'purification'. The poor think of it as a right to assistance: for wealthier Muslims it is a means of purification and spiritual enrichment.

In the early days of Islam the money was collected like ordinary taxes by government departments which were set up for the purpose, and in some countries today, e.g. Saudi Arabia and Pakistan, similar systems are used. Generally today, though, Muslims believe almsgiving is a personal matter, and it should be left to the individual to make appropriate arrangements to pay their zakat. Besides the giving of zakat, all Muslims, whether wealthy or poor, help those in need throughout the year by giving donations of money, by doing good and by offering love and sympathy.

The Fourth Pillar: Fasting

Fasting is considered an important part of Muslim life. Muslims are instructed to fast throughout Ramadan, the ninth month of their year. The rule says that during the hours of daylight they cannot eat or drink at all on any day of the whole month. Neither must they smoke or have sexual intercourse. This is a great test of self-control, and it aims first to teach Muslims restraint and self-discipline. It also shows, as a result of being hungry, that they can appreciate their own good fortune in life and share in the sufferings of those who are not so fortunate. Some Muslims are excused the fast, e.g. old people, the sick, pregnant women, children under the age of ten and those travelling on journeys. The latter must make up any time they did not fast at a later date. At the end of the month there is a time of celebration, i.e. the festival of Id-ul-Fitr.

The Muslim Year

The year consists of twelve months and it is calculated according to the movement of the moon. This means that each Muslim month has twenty-nine days which is the time from one new moon to the next. As the Muslim year is shorter than the year followed by most people in the world, the month of Ramadan occurs a few days earlier in the seasons year by year. Ramadan, therefore, occasionally falls in the summer, and in the Middle Eastern countries especially, when the days are long and hot, the fast is a severe test.

The Fifth Pillar: Pilgrimage

As far as possible all Muslims go on pilgrimage to Mecca at least once in their lifetime. Only those who are physically handicapped or simply cannot afford it because they are so poor, are excused. Many Muslims save money over several years in order to make the journey.

Every year over a million Muslims make the pilgrimage which takes place in the twelfth month (Dhu-al-Hijjah). Everyone finds it an enriching experience as they meet in fellowship with Muslims from many different countries. Up to two million pilgrims can visit Mecca in one week.

The Muslim name for the pilgrimage is Hajj. While on pilgrimage a man wears white robes made from two pieces of cotton cloth. Women wear a simple white gown and a white head covering. Since all wear the same clothing, from the very rich to the poor, from the humble to those in positions of authority, there is a great sense of unity and equality. The pilgrimage lasts for about fourteen days and when it is over the pilgrim is called a 'hajji', which means 'one who has been on pilgrimage to Mecca'.

The pilgrims must follow a definite route and carry out special duties in and around the city of Mecca. Many places which are associated with Muhammad are visited.

The Ka'ba

The pilgrim first visits the Ka'ba which is situated in the great central courtyard of the Great Mosque. He must touch and kiss the Black Stone which is set in an outside wall of the temple. Then he walks round the temple seven times in an anticlockwise direction, that is with his left shoulder nearest the building. This event is called Tawaf.

Abraham's Shrine

Next comes a visit to Abraham's shrine which was built near the Ka'ba. The shrine commemorates Abraham and his son, Ishmael, who, tradition says, built the Ka'ba.

The Sa'y (the 'Running')

The next duty involves running, from one side to the other, along the length of a broad street. This connects two small hills, Safa and Marwa, in the centre of Mecca. It recalls Hagar's search for water for her son, Ishmael, after her husband Abraham had left them both there in the desert. Tradition says Ishmael found a spring of water which now feeds a well. The well is called Zam Zam and pilgrims drink from it during the Hajj.

Mount Arafat

On the ninth day the pilgrim journeys some thirteen miles across the desert to Mount Arafat where Muhammad preached. He climbs the mountain (called the Mount of Mercy) to confess his sins to God, and he joins in the the noon and the mid-afternoon prayers. He then goes back towards Mecca

Pilgrims at Mina

and spends the night camping out under the stars at Muzdalifah after saying the evening prayers. On this section of the pilgrimage many pilgrims walk all the way from Mecca and back again.

Mina

The following day he travels to Mina, a village five miles from Mecca. Here he throws seven stones at three tall pillars. This recalls the time when Abraham drove away the devil by throwing stones at him, and it symbolizes the pilgrim's intention to give up evil.

Following the stoning, an animal, usually a sheep, is bought and slaughtered. It reminds Muslims of how God provided Abraham with a ram to sacrifice instead of his son. Some of the meat is eaten, and the remainder is given to the poor. Muslims throughout the world join in this sacrifice as this day is one of the feast days in the Muslim year, Id-ul-Adha.

The End of the Pilgrimage

On returning to Mecca the final duties are carried out. The pilgrim repeats the Tawaf and the Sa'y, and he drinks water from the Zam Zam well. Some take bottles of this water home for relatives and friends who have not been able to attend the pilgrimage. The white clothing that has been worn during the pilgrimage is carefully preserved since it will be used again as a shroud when the pilgrim dies.

The pilgrim then again dresses in his nor-

Muhammad's tomb at Medina, from a picture in the Islamic Centre, Leicester

mal clothes and returns home. Many stay a little longer to visit Muhammad's tomb, the magnificent mosque in Medina and other important sites of Islam.

The Lesser Pilgrimage
There is also a less important pilgrimage which anyone going to Mecca at any other time of the year can undertake. Muslims carry this out because it was Muhammad's practice whenever he went to Mecca. It involves putting on Inram, i.e. the white clothing, on the outskirts of the city, and then performing a Tawaf and a Sa'y, as is done on the Hajj.

8 The Muslim Holy Books

The Name of the Book
Muslims call their most holy book, the Qur'an. This name means 'recitation'. It is a collection of the messages which Muhammad said the Archangel Gabriel revealed to him. Muslims believe these sayings are the actual words of Allah. Gabriel appeared to Muhammad on many occasions and, since he could neither read nor write, Muhammad had to recite the messages until he could remember them by heart. He then passed the teaching on when he preached to the people.

The Compilation of the Qur'an
During Muhammad's lifetime many sayings which he received from the angel were written down. Often, after a revelation, Muhammad asked his secretary, Zaid, to write down the message while it was still fresh in

his mind. Zaid had to use whatever material was available at the time, so at first parts of

The Qur'an

the Qur'an were written on paper, wood, leather and even bone! No complete copy of the Qur'an was written down until after Muhammad's death. All his companions put together the teachings they had learned by heart with all the parts already written, and a complete book was compiled. The Third Rightly-guided Caliph, Uthman, had an authoritative copy produced around AD 650, and it was sent to the main Islamic cities including Jerusalem, Damascus and Babylon. Within a few years it was accepted as the genuine record of the teaching of Allah as given to Muhammad by the angel. It has not been changed in any way since that time.

The Form of the Qur'an
The book is written in Arabic, and consists of many chapters which are called 'suras'. There are 114 suras altogether, and all are written in verse. Except for the first sura, they are arranged in the order of the longest to the shortest. The whole book is about the same length as the New Testament of the Bible. Instead of using numbers each sura has been given a name, e.g. 'Mary', 'Salvation', 'The Prophets', 'Joseph', etc.

The Contents of the Qur'an
The book gives guidance to Muslims on all aspects of their faith. On spiritual affairs it shows Muslims how to live in submission to Allah, and explains that they must show repentence and accept the judgment of Allah.

There is guidance on everyday living, for instance, on the sharing of possessions, the duties of parents and employers, and the treatment of women and orphans as well as an outline of the laws concerning marriage and divorce. As far as marriage is concerned, the Qur'an teaches that it is permitted for a man to marry up to four wives, but they must all be treated equally and fairly; if this should be impossible, then a man must have only one wife. The Qur'an forbids the drinking of alcohol and the practice of gambling of any sort. Also it is forbidden to practice usury, that is charging interest when lending money.

The Qur'an includes many references to great prophets and people of the past. For instance, there are stories about Abraham, Jacob, Joseph, and Mary, the mother of Jesus. Through such passages Muslims learn much about Allah and His nature, the Last Judgment, the Life Hereafter, angels and the messengers of Allah, His Prophets.

The Place of the Qur'an in Worship
The book is greatly revered by Muslims as the actual word of God. Passages from it are learned by heart and used as prayers each day. The first sura is frequently used at the beginning of prayer; this gives an outline of the Muslim belief in one God, the One who judges and guides men at all times. Also during the Friday noon prayer in the mosque the Imam may give a sermon and he

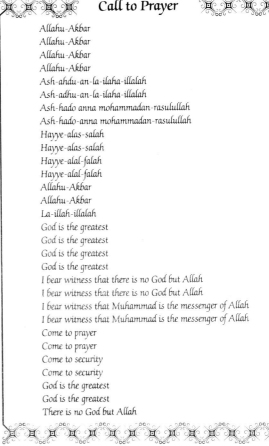

Call to Prayer

Allahu-Akbar
Allahu-Akbar
Allahu-Akbar
Allahu-Akbar
Ash-ahdu-an-la-ilaha-illalah
Ash-adhu-an-la-ilaha-illalah
Ash-hado anna mohammadan-rasulullah
Ash-hado-anna mohammadan-rasulullah
Hayye-alas-salah
Hayye-alas-salah
Hayye-alal-falah
Hayye-alal-falah
Allahu-Akbar
Allahu-Akbar
La-illah-illalah
God is the greatest
God is the greatest
God is the greatest
God is the greatest
I bear witness that there is no God but Allah
I bear witness that there is no God but Allah
I bear witness that Muhammad is the messenger of Allah
I bear witness that Muhammad is the messenger of Allah
Come to prayer
Come to prayer
Come to security
Come to security
God is the greatest
God is the greatest
There is no God but Allah

The 'adhan' or call to prayer

may use a passage from the Qur'an as the basis of his message.

Hadith

Besides the Qur'an, Muslims use a book called Hadith (meaning 'sayings'). It contains the words of advice and guidance spoken by Muhammad. These help to explain and interpret the Qur'an which on many matters gives only an outline. The words of Hadith do not have the authority and reverence of the Qur'an, but as Muhammad is regarded as a perfect example of a Muslim, his teachings and explanations are greatly respected. Hadith therefore acts as a supplement to the teachings found in the Qur'an. As an example of Hadith teaching, the book declares 'that a man must bathe every week, he must wash his head and his whole body', yet the Qur'an's instruction regarding cleanliness is that a Muslim should wash before praying.

9 Important Events in a Muslim's Life

Throughout a Muslim's lifetime there are a number of ceremonies which have particular importance; these are carried out at birth, a week later (the naming ceremony), at the age of four, on being married, and finally when a Muslim dies.

At Birth

Within a few minutes of birth the 'adhan' (the call to prayer) is spoken to the baby. Either the father or another member of the family stands in front of the baby, and calls out the words into the baby's ear as an act of blessing. Occasionally a learned member of the Muslim community is asked to carry out the ceremony on behalf of the family.

The Naming Ceremony

A week after a baby's birth, the family and their friends gather for the naming ceremony. The baby is named by the father after passages from the Qur'an have been recited. Male babies are circumcised on this day (cf. Judaism, page 34) and the baby's head is shaved as a symbol that the child is rid of all misfortune. The child's hair is weighed and an equivalent weight of gold and silver is given to charity.

The 'Bismillah' Ceremony

This takes place when a child is exactly four years, four months and four days old. It is a commemoration of the first occasion that the Angel Gabriel appeared to Muhammad, and it marks the beginning of the child's religious training. On the day the child receives a gift of sweets.

The child's training takes place in the Madressa ('the school at the mosque') which he or she attends regularly from that time. It is there that all Muslim children learn Arabic so that they can read and understand the Qur'an; many passages from the book are learned by heart. They are also taught how to say their prayers and how to carry out the ritual that is performed when they pray.

Marriage

In Islam most marriages are arranged by the parents, but nowadays the agreement of the young couple for their marriage is often sought as well. Marriage is a civil contract in Islam but it is regarded as a mutual agreement made between the man and the woman before God and men.

The wedding ceremony can be simple or elaborate, and it is attended by the couple's relations and friends. Any convenient place is used for the signing of the marriage contract. Usually a respected Muslim officiates; often it is the Imam.

At the ceremony the Imam will recite some appropriate passages from the Qur'an, and then give an address on the meaning of marriage, and on the responsibilities and rights of the husband and wife; finally he will pray for God's blessing on the couple. The marriage vows are made by the couple, and both of them sign the written contract. The groom always presents his bride with a gift, usually of money. This gift is the wife's by right and it can never be claimed by her husband.

Although the Qur'an teaches that a man may have up to four wives, nowadays few Muslims have more than one wife. Divorce is possible in the Muslim faith but it is not regarded with favour. Great efforts are always made by the couple's families and their friends to bring about a reconciliation in any marriage breakdown before a final divorce is agreed. Muslim law lays down a strict procedure which must be followed, and it may be more than a year before a final separation takes place.

The Funeral Ceremony

In the Muslim faith there are a number of rites that take place at the time of a person's death. When a Muslim is dying he will, if possible, say the Shahada. Relatives and friends come to the dead person's house to offer comfort to the family. They recite parts of the Qur'an and pray for God's mercy on the person who has died.

The funeral ceremony is simple and takes place as soon as possible after death. After the corpse has been washed (always by members of the same sex), it is wrapped in clean white sheets and then placed in a coffin. If possible the white clothes worn by the dead person on pilgrimage to Mecca are used. The coffin is taken to the mosque where funeral prayers are said by relatives and friends. The burial then takes place in the cemetery; Muslims are always buried with their faces towards Mecca. A period of mourning follows which may last as long as forty days.

Muslims have a strong belief in Life after Death and in a Day of Judgment when all their actions will be judged. They say that God will reward the faithful by allowing them to go to Paradise where they will enjoy peace and happiness. However those who have disobeyed God will go to Hell. In this way all will be rewarded or punished according to what they have done during their lives on earth.

10 Festivals

In Islam there are six annual celebrations. Muhammad himself introduced the two festivals of Id-ul-Fitr and Id-ul-Adha. Besides these, there are four occasions when historical events in the life of Muhammad are remembered—the Day of the Hijra (1st Muharram and New Year's Day), the Birthday of Muhammad (12th Rabi'ul-Awwal), the Night of Power (Lailat-ul-Qadr) and the Night of the Journey (Lailat-ul-Isra).

Id-ul-Fitr

(The Little Feast or the Festival of Fast Breaking)
This is a three-day festival to mark the end of the fast of Ramadan. It is a very joyful community and family occasion when everyone wears their best clothes. In the morning all Muslim families flock to the mosques to take part in communal prayers. They thank God for all the blessings they have received as a result of keeping the fast and for the gift of God's message written in the Qur'an. They also seek God's mercy and forgiveness and ask for continued strength to live by the Qur'an.

During the festival a type of welfare tax is paid by the head of the family on behalf of all the members of the household. This is called Sadaquah a-Fitr and it is given to the poorer members of the community so that they can take part in the festivities.

Throughout the day the celebrations are enjoyed by everyone. Visits are made to the homes of relatives and friends, and parties are held. It is a special day for children who are given presents, sweets and new clothes. Delicious meals are prepared; these include a favourite dessert—a sweet pudding with dates and milk. Everyone exchanges Id

An Id greeting card, showing the alternative 'Eid' spelling

greetings cards, and people greet each other saying 'Id-Mubarak' ('Happy Id') and 'Assalama Alaykum' ('the peace of God be with you'). Also on this day many visit family graves to say prayers for their departed relatives.

Generally the festival is an outward expression of the unity of family solidarity, and a time for prayer, for giving thanks and for seeking forgiveness.

Id-ul-Adha

(The Great Feast or the Festival of Sacrifice) This is the festival of sacrifice which begins on the tenth day of the pilgrimage to Mecca and it lasts two to three days. Muslims who are not on the pilgrimage also join in the celebrations wherever they live in the world; in this way the unity of all Muslims is emphasized. For Muslims, the festival commemorates the willingness of Abraham to sacrifice his son, Ishmael, as an act of obedience to God's will, and it symbolizes their own willingness to sacrifice their lives and property in the name of God and for the cause of Islam.

On the first day Muslims wear their best clothes and attend congregational prayers in the mosque. Those who can afford it sacrifice an animal, e.g. a sheep; often several families share one animal. The animal is slaughtered in the prescribed way while prayers from the Qur'an are spoken. (In Britain special arrangements are made for the animals to be slaughtered by Muslims in abattoirs.) Before the meat from these animals is eaten all the blood must be drained away; meat prepared in this way is called 'halal'. The meat is distributed amongst the family and their friends, but one third must be given to the poor. Like Id-ul-Fitr, the festival is a time of visiting friends and relatives, and exchanging greetings and gifts.

The Day of the Hijra

(1st Muharram and New Year's Day) On 1st Muharram Muslims celebrate Muhammad's migration ('the Hijra') from Mecca to Medina. For Muslims the Hijra is one of the most significant events in their history since it was in Medina that Islam was first established as an important religion to spread rapidly over the next few centuries. It is also remembered as the first day of the New Year, and so it is an occasion for exchanging greetings and relating stories about Muhammad and his companions, i.e. his first converts to Islam who fled with him to Medina.

Preparing animals for slaughter for Id-ul-Adha

The Birthday of Muhammad
(12th Rabi'ul-Awwal)
Muslims celebrate the 12th of Rabi'ul-Awwal as Muhammad's birthday; in fact the whole month is celebrated as 'the birth month' of the prophet. Muslims consider the birth of Muhammad as the most important event in world history, since they believe he is the last and greatest of all the prophets. Muslims everywhere remember the birthday by meeting together and relating stories of Muhammad's life. They also think about the quality of Muhammad's life and they are exhorted to follow his example in their daily living.

The Night of Power
(Lailat-ul-Qadr)
In the Qur'an the night on which Muham-

mad first received God's message from the Angel Gabriel is called the Night of Power. The event is celebrated on the 27th Ramadan, and on this night Muslims spend a considerable time reading the Qur'an and saying prayers. Muhammad himself is said to have spent more time during the last ten nights of Ramadan in private devotion than at any period of the year.

The Night of the Journey
(Lailat-ul-Isra)
According to Muslim tradition Muhammad made a journey one night from the Ka'ba in Mecca to the remains of Solomon's Temple in Jerusalem. From this spot Muhammad is said to have ascended to heaven where he saw many signs of God. This experience is described in the Qur'an in sura 17 verse 1.

On the same night God instructed Muhammad to instruct his followers to observe the five obligatory daily periods of prayer.

Muslims say this event took place in the tenth year of Muhammad's prophethood during the night of 27th Rajab. Muslims remember the occasion by reading the Qur'an and saying additional prayers.

In Jerusalem the famous mosque called the Dome of the Rock is built over the rock from which Muslims say Muhammad ascended to heaven on this particular night.

A Shi'a Festival

Amongst the Shi'a Muslims the first ten days of Muharram are an important time of commemoration. They remember the martyrdoms of Ali, the 4th Rightly-guided Caliph, and his sons, Hasan and Husain. The Shi'a remember them as being the only true leaders of Islam since they were members of Muhammad's family (see page 57).

In Shi'a towns before the festival begins black tents, decorated with Shi'a symbols, are set up in the streets. People wearing mourning clothes meet in the tents to hear the story of Husain. It is a very emotional occasion, the audience wails and weeps as the story unfolds. Finally a passion play re-enacting the suffering, the martyrdom, and the burial of Husain in Karbala is performed.

The Dome of the Rock

·Glossary·

Adhan	call to prayer made by the muezzin (cf. page 66)
Allah	Muslim name for God (cf. page 53)
Bismillah	ceremony held in infancy to mark the beginning of a child's religious training (cf. page 67)
Caliph	ruler of the Islamic Empire in the years following Muhammad (cf. page 56)
Du'ah	informal and private prayer (cf. page 61)
Hadith	book containing a record of the deeds and sayings of Muhammad (cf. page 67)
Hajj	pilgrimage to Mecca (cf. page 63)
Hajji	person who has undertaken the pilgrimage to Mecca (cf. page 64)
Hijra	'migration' of Muhammad from Mecca to Medina (cf. page 55)
Id-ul-Adha	festival held to remember Abraham's willingness to sacrifice his son Ishmael (cf. page 69)
Id-ul-Fitr	festival held to mark the end of the fast of Ramadan (cf. page 68)
Imam	leader of the local Muslim community; conducts prayers in the mosque (cf. page 59)
Islam	name of the Muslim religion; means 'submission to Allah' (cf. page 53)
Ka'ba	sacred building in the centre of Mecca (cf. page 59)
Khadija	wife of Muhammad (cf. page 54)
Kiswa	large cloth covering put on the Ka'ba (cf. page 59)
Madressa	'school' at the mosque where Muslim children have their religious training (cf. page 67)
Mecca	Muslim holy city in Arabia; centre of the Muslim faith (cf. page 54)
Medina	holy city in Arabia to which Muhammad migrated and where he set up the first Muslim community (cf. page 55)
Mihrab	recess in the mosque wall which indicates the direction of Mecca (cf. page 58)
Minaret	tall tower on a mosque from which the muezzin calls people to pray (cf. page 58)
Minbar	small preaching stand in the mosque (cf. page 58)
Muezzin	official who calls the Muslim people to prayer from minaret (cf. page 58)
Muhammad	the Prophet who revealed the Islamic faith (cf. page 53)
Muharrum	first month of the Muslim year; an important time of celebration for Shi'a Muslims (cf. page 71)
Muslim	'one who has surrendered to Allah'; a follower of the Muslim faith (cf. page 53)
Qibla	means 'direction'; the wall in the mosque in which the mihrab is placed (cf. page 58)
Qur'an	the Muslim holy book (cf. page 65)

Rak'ah	a complete sequence of movements followed in Salat prayer (cf. page 62)
Ramadan	the ninth month in the Muslim year; the month of fasting (cf. page 63)
Salat	a Pillar of Islam; the set pattern of prayer to be performed five times each day (cf. page 61)
Shahada	the first Pillar of Islam; the Muslim statement of faith (cf. page 60)
Shi'a	an important branch of Islam, the followers of Ali, the 4th Rightly-guided Caliph; also called Shi'ites (cf. page 57)
Sunni	name of the main branch of Islam or a follower of it (cf. page 57)
Zakat	the third Pillar of Islam; almsgiving; the tax by which Muslims give money to charity (cf. page 63)

·Activities·

1 Important Things to Remember and Understand

Special words and ideas: Allah; Hajj; hijra; Imam; Islam; Muslim; Muhammad; Qur'an; Salat; shahada; zakat.

2 Important Things to Find Out

Interview a Muslim who has been on the pilgrimage to Mecca and ask him about the experience.
Find out in what ways Islam has helped to broaden man's knowledge in science and medicine.
Talk to Muslim young people to discover what they think of their way of life.

3 Important Things to Discuss

Do the actions of fundamental Muslim governments, e.g. Iran, Pakistan, present a favourable image of Islam to the world?
Discuss the role of women in Islam.
Is it difficult, or even impossible, for a strict Muslim to live in a Western country?

4 Important Things to Do

Draw a chart illustrating the Five Pillars of Islam.
Study Muslim calligraphy (handwriting) and try to copy some examples.
Visit a mosque and ask the Imam to talk about the building and how it is used.

5 Written Work

a Describe and comment on the main ceremonies that take place in a Muslim's life.
b Describe and comment on the Five Pillars of Islam.
c Which events in Muhammad's life ensured that Islam developed into an important world religion?

CHAPTER 4

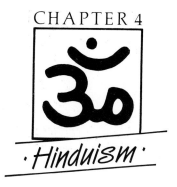

·Hinduism·

1 What is Hinduism?

The word 'Hinduism' stands for the faith and the way of life of most of the people who live in India. 'Hind' is the name given by the Persians to the River Indus and to the area around the river in North-west India; in time the word 'Hindu' came to mean 'Indian'. Hinduism has no creed and no founder. It has no recognizable beginning: it is a religion that has slowly developed over a period of time.

Hinduism is such an ancient religion that intermingled within it are many types of beliefs and religious practices. Originally there were no priests or temples; people in a simple way offered gifts to the forces of nature, e.g. water, wind, sun, etc. in the open air. Around 1750 BC Aryan invaders from Central Asia settled in North-west India and introduced their own religious ideas which were written in their holy book, the Veda. The Aryans also brought the idea of the caste system (see page 77), which is still an important aspect of the Hindu way of life.

Hindus slowly came to accept the idea of the existence of an Eternal Supreme Being. They call this being, Brahman. To help them understand, Hindus worship different gods which individually represent one particular aspect of Brahman. The most popular of these lesser gods are Brahma, the creator, Vishnu, the preserver, and Shiva, the destroyer.

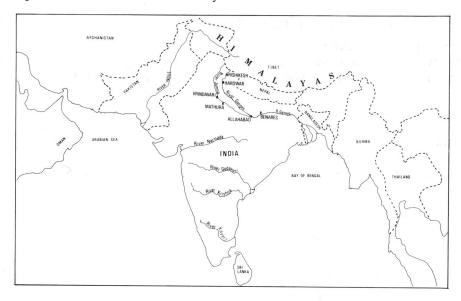

India

2 Beliefs of the Hindus

Since Hinduism developed slowly over many centuries, and since, unlike the other major religions in the world, it has no founder, its main beliefs and religious ideas are varied and are not always accepted by all who call themselves Hindus. However there are some common ideas which all Hindus accept; these concern the gods, life before and after death, and the caste system which governs a Hindu's place in society.

The Hindu Gods

All Hindus believe that Brahman is the origin and the sustainer of all life, and the goal of all living things. They believe Brahman is eternal and omnipotent, and only he is real. Part of Brahman is in all living things; this is 'atman', and it is sometimes referred to as the soul. As Brahman is so great he cannot be explained in human words because all humans are imperfect and Brahman is perfect. Also as Brahman is beyond ordinary understanding, Hindus worship hundreds of gods; each one representing one particular aspect of Brahman.

Of all the multitude of gods, three are worshipped more than the others, these are Brahma, Vishnu and Shiva. Brahma, the creator god, is portrayed with four heads, each facing in a different direction, and four arms. This is to show that he has knowledge of all things in the universe. Vishnu is the preserver of all life, and the god of goodness and love. In order to protect the world from disasters, Hindus say that Vishnu has appeared on earth in ten different forms, for instance as a fish, a tortoise, a boar, as Prince Rama and Krishna. When a God appears on earth in a different form in this way he is called an 'avatar'. Shiva is the god who destroys things so that new things can grow in their place. Pictures portray him as a frightening figure, often as Lord of the Dance dancing the dance of destruction and creation.

Taken together these three gods recall the Hindu idea that Brahman creates the

Brahma, Vishnu and Shiva (left to right)

universe, continually sustains it while it is in being, and in the course of time destroys it. Following a period of rest Brahman recreates the universe, and so begins again the endless cycle of creation and destruction. Occasionally Brahma, Vishnu and Shiva are represented as one god with three faces. Hindus call this form the Trimurti and occasionally the Hindu Trinity.

Life Before and After Death

A Hindu believes and hopes that eventually his soul will join with Brahman and, when this happens, he will find perfect peace and happiness. So he welcomes death as a step nearer to gaining this everlasting union with Brahman. Also he believes his soul, being part of Brahman, is never born and never dies, but moves on from one body to another. This movement of the soul from one body to another in the cycle of birth, death and re-birth, is called reincarnation. This belief that a person will be born again following death is linked with the law of karma. The type of existence a person will experience in the next life depends on the good and bad karma built up in the previous life.

Since Hindus believe that 'atman', or the soul, is in all living things, they treat animals with great respect and take great care of them. The white cow is especially sacred because it is the symbol of 'atman'. These animals are not harmed even though they could be used as food, and they are allowed to roam the towns and countryside without interference. This idea of non-violence to animals applies to people as well. It is an ancient Hindu idea, and it is called 'ahimsa'.

The Caste System

The caste system has been a very important part of Hinduism since the early days of the faith. It was introduced by the Aryans when they settled in North-west India. In the holy books of the Aryans, the Vedas, the legend of Purusha explains the origin of the caste system. The legend tells how Brahma made the first man, Purusha. Later Purusha was sacrificed and from his body four different

groups or castes were taken. The high caste, the Brahmins (the priests), came from his mouth; from his arms, the warriors or rulers called Kshatriyas; the skilled workers and traders, the Vaisyas, came from his thighs; and finally, the unskilled labourers and servants, called the Shudras, from his feet. Over the centuries many sub-castes have grown up until today there are many hundreds of them. In practice a member of a 'high' caste is considered purer than those below him, and a member of a 'low' caste is impure.

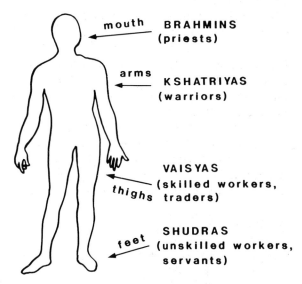

The relationship of caste and Purusha

A caste is therefore a group of people with a particular place in society. Hindu people are born into their caste, whether high or low, and they must accept their place without question. This means that a person can only be born a Hindu. To maintain purity Hindus only marry within their caste, can only eat with members of their own caste, and the men follow occupations of their caste which are passed on from father to son. Some people are unclean because of their occupations, e.g. barbers, butchers, tanners; they must belong to low castes. On the other hand, Brahmins, the priests, are in the high pure caste, and they must keep clean since they approach gods in worship and handle sacred things.

Hindu family ties are very strong. All relatives in a family have to undergo a period of purification after a birth or a death because, Hindus say, such things cause pollution. The whole family is also polluted if any member does polluting work. Therefore occupations tend to run in families as people want to protect their families from pollution.

There is a large group of people who are outside the caste system; they are referred to in various ways, e.g. untouchables or outcastes. They are among the poorest and least educated people in India and they do all the dirtiest jobs. There have been some attempts to improve the lot of the untouchables. The great Indian leader, Gandhi, took up their cause and even called them the 'harijans' which means 'children of God'. The Indian Government has passed laws against classifying people as 'untouchables', but customs die hard and there is still much discrimination and hostility against them.

But things are changing in modern India. In the cities, because of factory and office work and through the use of public transport and restaurants, the contact with strangers means that the rules of purity are breaking down and caste rules are being relaxed. However, in the country villages where life has changed very little, the caste rules are still observed just as they have been for centuries.

3 Rituals of Life in Hinduism

There is no initiation rite in Hinduism by which a person becomes a Hindu. However there is a series of rituals called samskaras, which prepare a Hindu for a new phase in life. These rituals begin with the conception of a child and they continue through life to cremation following death. The most important of these samskaras are naming a child, the giving of the sacred thread, marriage, and the funeral ceremony.

Rituals Concerning the Beginning of Life
In the early days of marriage, even before children are conceived, parents pray for and meditate on the kind of child they wish to have. During pregnancy a number of rites are performed when the gods are asked to protect the unborn child, and to strengthen the mother spiritually, mentally and physically so that a healthy child is born.

Name-giving
On the eleventh or twelfth day after birth a name is chosen for the baby. The choice of name is very important; it must be auspicious, i.e. one which it is hoped will bring good fortune. Often the name is that of a god, goddess or hero, e.g. Rama or Krishna for boys and Durga or Sita for girls. A boy's name may indicate heroism, e.g. Vijaya—'victory' and a girl's name may indicate beauty, e.g. Lalita—'charming'. Some babies are named Devadatta ('given by the god') or Deviprasada ('favour of the goddess'). These show that the parents believe their child was given to them by the favour of a particular god, or that the parents have dedicated their child to a god. Parents would choose such names as a result of praying and making vows to the god in the hope that they would have a child.

The name is given in a very simple way. The father leans over the baby and says into its ear, 'Now your name is . . .'.

The Thread Ceremony
This ceremony is a very important stage in the life of a Hindu boy, that is, if he belongs to one of the three main castes, i.e. Brahmins, Kshatriyas, Vaisyas (for castes see page 77). These castes are called 'twice-born' because the thread ceremony is considered a birth by which a person is given a new kind of life. The ceremony takes place at any time between the seventh and twelfth birthdays of a boy. It involves putting on the sacred thread, a loop of cotton string which hangs over the left shoulder and across the

body to the right hip. Once he has received the thread a boy has the right to recite passages from the Veda and perform the rituals described in it.

The actual ceremony takes place in a garden by a sacrificial fire. The boy's guru, or teacher, who has prepared him for the ceremony, presents the thread to him, and then he prays that the boy continues growing in his spiritual life. The boy has now been born into full membership of his caste, and he accepts all the responsibilities that go with it. In fact from a religious point of view he has become a man.

The boy begins his new life by studying the Veda of ancient Hindu literature (see page 87) under the guidance of his guru. The guru is regarded as a second father to the boy and he must be respected even more than his natural father. Most boys do not learn much of the Veda; usually just a verse called the Gayatri Mantra. Thus the time of study is not long, though some boys study the Veda for several years. The boy is now prepared for the next stage in his life, i.e. marriage.

Marriage

It is very important for a man to be married since it enables him to have sons who will continue his family line. Many Hindu marriages are arranged, which means parents find suitable partners for their children. Parents always take care to find a suitable partner from the same caste, and they make sure that the young people's horoscopes are a good match.

The Engagement Ceremony

This is a happy occasion when the young couple's parents announce the forthcoming marriage. The men of both families sit facing the girl while a priest reads from a holy book. (The women of both families sit in a separate room, but the young man is not present.) After the reading and the chanting of mantras and prayers has finished the young woman bows repeatedly to the men. The ceremony ends with the priest passing round food which has been specially prepared for the betrothal. Throughout the proceedings a band of musicians plays lively tunes in keeping with the occasion.

A traditional Hindu wedding ceremony. The curtain hides the bride and bridegroom from each other until the couple are pronounced man and wife

The Marriage Ceremony

A marriage is a great family occasion and many guests are invited. The ceremony itself lasts about an hour, but the celebrations can last up to five days. There are several feasts, and the young couple visit the local shrine to ask for a blessing from the god.

The wedding ceremony begins as soon as the bridegroom arrives at his bride's house. He comes in a procession. He may ride on a horse or be carried on a special chair by a group of friends. At the bride's house a small fire burns in a brazier. The priest keeps the fire burning by pouring clarified butter, called ghee, on the flames. He also puts spices and rice on the fire; this is to promote fertility. The bride is veiled and usually wears a fine new white sari. The bridegroom wears a new suit and a gold turban. Both of them wear garlands of brightly-coloured flowers round their necks—sometimes nowadays paper flowers are used. The most important part of the ceremony is the seven steps when the groom leads his bride round the fire seven times. To symbolize the couple being joined together in marriage one end of a bright pink sari is put round the bridegroom's neck and the other end is tied to the bride's sari. Then the bridegroom's mother puts a red and green sari over the bride's head as a sign that she is welcomed into the family. The priest conducting the ceremony takes a thread from this sari and ties the wrists of the bridegroom's parents together showing that they will be responsible for the bride. The bride now leaves her home and goes with her husband to become part of his family.

The Funeral Ceremony

The last of the important samskaras takes place when a person dies. A funeral ceremony is held at which the body of the dead person is cremated.

When a person dies their body is wrapped in a cloth and then taken away for cremation. In the countryside there is a cremation ground outside the village where the body is placed on a pyre of sweet-smelling sandalwood. In Indian cities and in the

Funeral pyres beside the River Ganges in Benares

Western world, however, Hindus use the modern crematorium for burning their dead. Prayers are said and the closest relative lights the fire, e.g. the eldest son lights his father's funeral pyre. Most of the relatives leave before the cremation is over, but the closest relative remains until the cremation is over in order to collect the ashes and bones. These are later scattered in a river, preferably the holy River Ganges.

No refreshments are served after a funeral, as eating must always be kept separate from anything to do with death. The family and other mourners return home after the funeral and have a bath. When they have a meal after attending a funeral they will not eat any sweet food. Great care is taken to make sure that funerals are conducted correctly, otherwise, Hindus believe, bad luck can come upon them.

4 Hindu Temples and Worship

The temple is the Hindu place of worship, and Hindus think of it as a house for the god which is worshipped there. Temples are dedicated to any of the many Hindu gods, and they are often situated at places where legends say gods appeared on earth or where miracles took place. Small temples are found in every village and town, but there are also some very large beautiful temples, many of which are found in South India. Priests officiate at ceremonies but ordinary Hindus can come and go as they please.

Small Temples
These are very simple structures about the same size as an ordinary house. They are usually built of wood or mud bricks. They

contain few rooms. The most important is the shrine room in which the image of the god is placed. There is also a small room for the priest's use. A veranda with steps leading up to it runs across the front of the temple. When the people come to worship at the temple they stand in the entrance to the shrine room on the veranda. Only the priest enters the shrine; he takes the gifts the people have brought and offers them to the image of the god. At the door there are some small bells which the priest rings to 'warn' the god that the people are coming to worship.

Large Temples
Large temples are very elaborate, having many rooms and courtyards. They are built of stone, and have towers which are covered with statues of the gods or with scenes portraying the legends associated with them. The most important part of the temple is the central shrine containing the image of the god. It is a small dark room with smooth uncarved walls, and it is situated at the west end of the temple. Above the shrine is a tall tower whose purpose is to cover the image respectfully, so giving it the honour its status deserves. The tower also represents a mountain which in many religions is regarded as sacred. In front of the shrine room is a large hall where people assemble, especially at festive times. At the entrance to the hall is a porch which faces east, the direction of the rising sun. In the courtyard by the porch stands a statue of an animal or bird

Worshippers prepare for a festival outside the temple

The Somnath Temple in Gujerat

which represents the creature on which the god of the temple rides in Hindu legends. This statue is regarded as the temple guardian. Around the main shrine there may be smaller shrines containing images of lesser gods. Some temples have a courtyard around the main central building, and over the entrances are built pyramid-shaped towers, again covered with many stone statues. Next to the temple or in the courtyard there may be a pool (usually called a tank) which is used for ritual bathing.

Some very large temples contain many more rooms. There are halls used for dancing, for schools and libraries, and for providing offices for temple administrators. Around the courtyards also there may be large sheds for storing the carts which are used in festival processions, and living quarters for all the temple staff. Temples also have extensive gardens where the flowers used in worship are grown so gardeners are also needed on the temple staff.

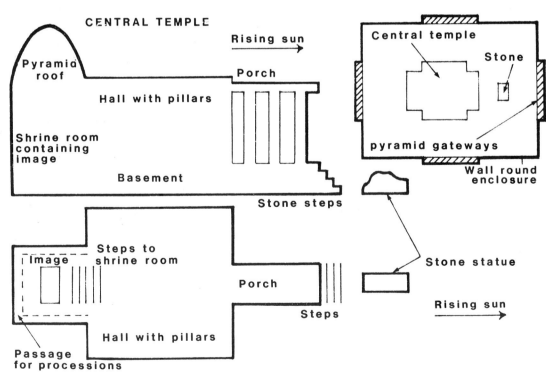

A plan of a Hindu temple

The Image

The image of the god occupies the centre of the shrine. It is made from wood, stone or bronze according to the rules laid down in Hindu holy books. The image, it is believed, has within it the life-force of the god it represents which will have entered during a special ceremony conducted by a Brahmin priest.

The image is therefore treated in a very special way, in fact as if it were the god himself. This is seen particularly in the temples in a daily ritual conducted by the priests. At dawn the god is 'woken up' in the bedroom where he has been asleep. The image is carried ceremoniously to the shrine room where it is washed, dried and dressed. Throughout the day the god is presented with offerings, fanned with elaborate fans, and entertained with music. At the end of the day the image is returned to its bedroom for the night.

A shrine room for Radha Krishna

Worship in the Temple

Individual Worship

Every temple, large and small, has priests. In the small village temples the priest may be part-time and a non-Brahmin. However the large temples have a full-time staff of Brahmins. The priest's task is to help those who come to worship and to act as an intermediary between the worshipper and the god represented by the image.

All worshippers must remove their shoes before entering the temple. Normally they remain in the main hall while a priest takes their offerings to the image. However, if they wish to enter the shrine, they must have a bath and change their clothes before doing so. Worship itself consists of offering gifts of food, flowers or clothing and saying prayers, and it takes place at the foot of the image. Any food offered to the god is later given to the worshippers to eat; it is then called 'prasada'. The image can also be worshipped by a priest waving a lamp containing many lights in front of it; this action is called 'arti'.

The offerings need not be expensive or elaborate, and they consist of such things as fruit, nuts, rice, water, flowers and threads of cloth. The worshippers know these are acceptable as long as they are offered sincerely and devoutly. Many Hindus object to using animals as offerings. They believe that 'atman', the life-force or soul (see page 76), is in all living things, and therefore they say it is wrong to sacrifice them. It is for this reason that many Hindus do not eat meat.

Communal Worship

Worship is often held in the temple in the presence of a congregation. It may combine three forms i.e. havan, arti, and the singing of bhajans (hymns). Havan is the offering of fire to the image. A priest kindles fire from small pieces of wood and camphor on a small portable altar. While passages from the Veda are chanted ghee and more wood are put on to the fire to keep it burning. Prayers for purity and to the main Hindu gods are offered. Prasada is also distributed to the congregation.

In arti the gods are worshipped by slowly waving a small flat tray containing five lights before the image. The tray is then taken amongst the worshippers who place gifts of money on it. The worshippers also hold their hands over the flames and pass them over their foreheads and hair. In this way they symbolically receive blessing and power from the gods. While arti is performed everyone sings hymns called bhajans. Some worshippers clap their hands in time to the music, and others play musical instruments like triangles and tambourines, and ring bells. During worship the foreheads of the worshippers are marked with a red dot showing that they have been blessed. (Many Hindu women put a red dot or bindi mark on their foreheads for decoration. This mark does not have any religious significance.)

The Function of the Temple
Its main function is as a place of worship. Local people constantly visit the temple to take their offerings. For many years temples have been the centre of community life. In years past they were the only place for public entertainment. At festival time they become theatres where plays and dances re-enacting the ancient legends of the gods are performed.

The large temples particularly provide employment for priests, musicians and gardeners since they are involved with the many rituals and ceremonies that are performed. In addition many temples own estates, and they need accountants to look after their business affairs.

Pilgrims visit some temples regularly and they give large amounts of money as offerings. This money is a valuable source of income and the temple authorities make great use of it. It is used to provide facilities for the pilgrims, to help with temple maintenance and build new temples, to help run schools and colleges and maintain hospitals, orphanages and homes for the poor, and to help support Hindu art and culture.

5 Form of Worship

The worship of the gods and the performance of religious rituals play a very important part in the daily lives of Hindus. Worship and ritual can be carried out alone, with the family, or in a large group, and they can be performed at home, on a river bank, or, as seen already, in a temple.

The Five Daily Obligations
The Brahmins, i.e. those of the highest and priestly caste, and others who wear the sacred thread, observe five obligations each day:

1 They must always worship Brahman, either directly, or through the other gods; the usual form of worship is 'puja'.

2 They must give reverence to the saints and holy men by reciting the Veda. Usually this consists of a repetition of the Gayatri Mantra (see page 85).

3 They must show proper respect for their parents and elders.

4 They must give shelter and alms to the poor or to holy men.

5 They are instructed to feed animals because Hindus believe all living things form one community.

Daily Rituals
By the many religious acts that are performed each day Hindus show that their religion affects their daily life to an enormous extent. Even the simplest actions, e.g. washing, sweeping the floor, preparing food and eating it, etc. are made into a ritual. A good idea of what is involved can be gained from the rituals a Hindu may carry out at the beginning of the day. As he rises from bed he places his right foot on the ground first in order to make a good start to the day. He says a prayer as his foot touches the ground which he believes was created

A Brahmin at prayer

ping. The best-known sayings are the sacred syllable 'Om', which represents the Supreme Being, Brahman (the Hindu word for 'Om' is shown at the beginning of the chapter), or the sacred verse called the Gayatri Mantra or the Mother of the Veda (see page 87). This is part of a hymn to the sun god Savitri; it says 'Let us meditate on the splendour of the god Savitri. May he stir our thoughts'. This mantra can be recited 108 times by counting on a string of 108 beads called a mala. He also uses other verses and mantras, especially those found in the Veda. A mantra is a verse, believed to have supernatural powers, used in ritual and meditation.

Puja

The most common form of worship performed by Hindus is puja; this is worshipping a god, using mantras and making offerings. Usually Hindus prefer to worship one particular god. This god is chosen according to their personal wish, or because of family tradition, or even because it is the main god of the area they live in but they may worship other gods as well.

In a Hindu house there is always a shrine where the family worships. It can be very

by God. He carefully cleans his teeth and tongue, and then has a bath using running water. This daily bath is very important since a Hindu must not eat any food or say his prayers without having a bath first. He may also put on his forehead the mark of the god he worships; for instance, three horizontal lines indicate the god Shiva, and three vertical lines, Vishnu. This is called a tilaka mark and it is usually made with red powder or paste.

The Brahmin Ceremony

A high-caste Hindu man, i.e. a Brahmin, may perform an elaborate ritual three times each day. The morning worship begins before sunrise. He sits facing east towards the sun (in the evening towards the west) in a cross-legged position in front of the image of the god he worships. He is stripped to the waist and his hair is tied in a knot. He sips water and sprinkles it round the image. He then carries out breathing exercises to aid his concentration. He prays by constantly repeating words and phrases, or by simply reciting the name of the god he is worship-

A Hindu family in Leicester performing puja

85

elaborate or very simple. It is usually just part of a room and often consists of a shelf on which the image is placed, surrounded by flowers. The most usual room in which to have the shrine is the kitchen.

Puja begins very early in the morning and continues intermittently throughout the day. The image is 'wakened up' with the lighting of a lamp, with the chanting of mantras and with the sound of music. The image is washed and anointed with ghee, i.e. clarified butter. It is touched with coloured powders, hung with garlands, and offered flowers. Incense is burned and arti is performed before the image. Some actions may be performed, especially anjali, which is done by putting the hands together and raising them up to the forehead or breast. Also a Hindu may kneel and place the forehead on the ground in front of the image. Both of these actions are acts of homage to the gods; they may also be performed to people as an act of respect. When doing the anjali to a person the words 'namaste' (meaning 'homage to you') may be spoken.

Yoga

This is a form of meditation which is practised by many Hindus. The word 'yoga' means 'yoking, disciplining', and it is a means of achieving mastery over the mind by means of exercises. The idea is to cut oneself off from the world and concentrate on Brahman, the Eternal.

In order to understand the purpose of yoga it is necessary to know about the law of karma. Hindus teach that karma decides what form a person will have in the next life. Karma, they say, is 'action done in a lifetime whether good or bad'. A devout Hindu tries to avoid building up bad deeds so as to total

as little 'bad' karma as possible. One way to do this is to cut himself off from the world and concentrate on Brahman by practising yoga. When using one method of yoga a Hindu will sit cross-legged on a firm surface in a comfortable but not too relaxed position. He keeps his back straight, and then, looking at the end of his nose, he begins his concentration exercises. In this way he cuts himself off from his physical surroundings to achieve union with Brahman. With this method he is aware of the world around, but it is out of focus, so it does not distract him. Thus the yogi (someone who practises yoga) uses yoga as a means of discovering Brahman within himself.

A yogi meditating. He is wearing the sacred thread over his left shoulder

6 Hindu Holy Books

Most of the world's major religions have just one holy book. However, there are several holy books in Hinduism which describe their beliefs, their legends and their religious practices. The most ancient is a collection of writings known as the Veda. Then there is an important law book called the Laws of Manu, and some literature, mostly poetry called the Epics.

The Veda

The Veda is the most ancient of all the books in Hindu literature. The word 'veda' means 'divine knowledge' and the three sections that make up the Veda were compiled some time between 1200 BC and 500 BC. This makes it the oldest religious writing in existence. At first its contents were passed down orally, and it was not put into a written form until the 15th century.

The first section consists of a collection of hymns dedicated to 33 gods, especially to Indr and Agni. The Rig-Veda, as it is called, meaning 'Veda of Praise', is the most important of the Vedic hymns. It consists of more than 1,000 hymns arranged in ten books called mandales, and each of these has a number of verses called mantras. These hymns are royal songs in praise of the many Hindu gods.

The Brahmanas is the name of the second section of the Veda. Like the other sections it is written in Sanskrit, the ancient language of the Hindus. Its name means 'belonging to the Brahmins'. It describes the various Vedic religious rites and ceremonies, and explains what they mean.

The third section of the Veda is called the Upanishads, which means 'sitting at the feet of the teacher'. It contains discussions, both in prose and verse, of the most important topics in the Hindu faith, e.g. Brahman, re-incarnation and the law of karma, and the creation.

The Laws of Manu

There are a number of Sanskrit law books in Hinduism; the best-known is the Laws of Manu which was written about 250 BC. According to Hindu legends Manu was one of the ancestors of mankind. The book shows how important Hindu beliefs are in everyday life. They give detailed instructions of what Hindus may or may not do.

The Epics

This is a collection of literature written after the Veda. It contains two very important poems, the Mahabarata and the Ramayana.

The Mahabarata is written in Sanskrit and contains 100,000 verses, making it the longest poem in the world. It is a description of the exploits of the heroes of the Hindu myths. The main part is the story of the battle between the armies of the two royal families, the Kauravas and the Pandavas. The most famous part is the Bhagavad-Gita, which consists of a discussion between Arjuna, one of the royal princes of the Pandavas, and his chariot driver, who is really Krishna in disguise, about the relationship of man with Brahman, and how man can achieve salvation.

The Ramayana is another long epic poem; it was written about AD 1 and describes the adventures of Prince Rama who, according to Hindu beliefs, is a re-incarnation of Vishnu. The story of Rama concerns his exile, and the rescue, with the help of Hanuman, the king of the monkeys, of his wife, Sita, who had been captured by a demon, Ravana. It is a favourite story of the Hindus, and it is frequently told through drama and dance at festival times.

The Hindu Books in Worship

Most of the hymns and prayers used when worshipping are taken from the Vedic hymns and the Upanishads. The most used verse is the mantra known as 'the Mother of the Veda' (see page 85). As Hindu worship is an individual thing, worshippers choose their own favourite passages and prayers when they do puja at the shrine at home or when they visit the local temple.

ॐ । भूः । भुवः । स्वः ॥
तत्सवितुर्वरेण्यम् ।
भर्गो देवस्य धीमहि ।
धियो यो नः प्रचोदयात् ॥

The Gayatri Mantra. The first line is the invocation, the remaining three lines are the mantra itself. 'Let us meditate on the excellent splendour of the god Savitri. May he stir our thoughts.'

7 Pilgrimage

A pilgrimage is a journey made by a follower to a holy city, shrine or temple, and going on pilgrimage plays an important part in Hinduism. There are a number of reasons for Hindus making a pilgrimage. They may wish to have a closer experience of the god they worship, or they may wish to wash away their sins by bathing in a holy river. Also they may intend to pray for favours already received. Besides this, the parents of a family may go to a place where a god is said to have appeared or to have performed miracles in order to pray for the birth of a child, or for a child to be cured of a long illness. Almost always a shrine or temple has been built on the spot where a god is believed to have appeared in visible form or where a miracle has occurred. There are many important places of pilgrimage in North India, and they are often associated with the River Ganges. The main centres are Rishikesh and Hardwar where the Ganges descends from the Himalayas, Vrindavan and Mathura on the River Jumna which are associated with the god Krishna, the meeting of the Rivers Ganges and Jumna at Allahabad and the most sacred of the Indian cities, Benares (also called Varenasi) on the Ganges. Besides the Ganges and the Jumna, many other rivers in India are considered sacred, for instance, the Narmada, the Godavari, the Krishna and the Kaveri. Hindus believe that a bath in a holy river washes away all their sins. They bathe from ghats which have been built on the river banks. A ghat is a series of steps leading down to the water's edge. The bodies of the dead are also cremated on the ghats.

There is no fixed time to go on pilgrimage. Many Hindus make a pilgrimage at festival

Religious bathing in the River Ganges in Benares

time. Kumbha Mela is a great bathing festival held once every twelve years during the month of Magh (January–February). The most important centre during the festival is Allahabad where the Ganges and the Jumna meet. Thousands and thousands of pilgrims pour into the area and live in rough huts and tents. There is one particular hour only when it is most propitious to bathe in the water, and when the greatest favours are bestowed by the gods. All the pilgrims aim to bathe at this time; it is said to be the largest crowd in the world.

When on pilgrimage Hindus usually take gifts with them to present to the god at the shrine in the place they are visiting. The gifts could be of money, produce, cloth, food or flowers. The pilgrims spend much of their time in worship both praying and bathing. The pilgrims also enjoy the visit. They wear their best clothes and eat festive food. They meet old friends, go sightseeing and buy souvenirs to take home.

8 Festivals

There are many festivals in the Hindu calendar which celebrate events or legends associated with the gods. Some festivals are held widely throughout India, but others are minor celebrations held in villages or small towns in remembrance of a local god. The main festivals are Navarati (called Durga-Puja in Bengal), Dasera, Diwali, Shivarati, Rama-navami or Janmashtami, and Holi.

Navarati

This nine-day festival is devoted to the goddess, Durga, the divine symbol of motherhood. It takes place at the end of the Indian year in late September or early October. Navarati means 'nine nights' and the celebrations take place mainly in the evenings. The story of Prince Rama (an avatar of Vishnu) is related in drama and dance in temples and public places. In the legend Rama lost his kingdom and his wife Sita was stolen from him by the demon Ravana. Seeking help in his attempt to rescue his wife, Rama prayed to Durga for seven days. On the eighth day he killed Ravana, and then made offerings of thanksgiving to Durga on the ninth day.

The tenth day, called Dasera, is the most eventful. It celebrates Rama's victory over Ravana. Bonfires are lit; fireworks and sparklers are set off. Effigies of Ravana are burned amidst general rejoicing. In Delhi huge celebrations are held at which an enormous effigy of Ravana over thirty metres high is burned, and there is a gigantic display of fireworks.

Besides this it is a time of social gatherings and family reunions. Families conduct puja to Rama and Sita. Rama represents security and protection from evil, and Sita, constancy and faithfulness. People are therefore reminded that good is more powerful than evil, and that they should be loyal and friendly to each other.

Durga-puja is the name given to these celebrations in Bengal. At this time the

Durga-puja—a portable shrine is taken round to bless the houses for the coming year

Chandi, a poem telling the story of the victory of Durga over the forces of evil, is related. It is a time, particularly, for newly-married daughters to leave their husbands' houses to pay visits to their parents at their family home. On the tenth day, the statue of Durga made for the period of the celebrations, and used as a focus of worship during the nine days, is taken in a joyful procession to a river bank and put into the water. As it sinks the people rejoice, believing that all unhappiness and ill-fortune have been carried away.

Diwali

This festival lasts for three or four days at the time of the new moon in late October or early November. In North India it marks the end of the old year and the beginning of the new.

At this time the people remember various stories about the gods. One of the most popular is taken from the Ramayana; it relates Rama and Sita's triumphal return to their kingdom, Ayodhya, and Rama's coronation. In Benares the entire story narrated in the Ramayana is told over a thirty-day period; it ends with a short pageant of Rama's victory procession. Another story concerns the goddess, Lakshmi, the consort of Vishnu, who visits houses lit by many lamps, bringing gifts and promising prosperity throughout the coming year to all those in the household.

Vishnu's defeat of the demon Bali is another reason for celebrating Diwali. According to the story, Bali gained control of the world; he then decided to perform a great sacrifice so that he could become the master of the heavens and the gods as well. Vishnu thought up a plan to defeat Bali. He took the form of a dwarf and went to beg for alms from Bali. Bali responded by offering Vishnu as much land as he could cover in three strides; thereupon Vishnu grew so large that he covered the world in two strides! Bali was therefore defeated, and he was banished, though Vishnu allowed him to rule the underworld; however he was permitted to return to earth for one day in the year, i.e. at Diwali.

Diwali is a celebration of the victory of light over darkness. The people brightly decorate and illuminate their homes as well as the temples, streets and shops. Rows of little oil lamps light up the garden paths of the houses. Even the working animals are

A Hindu family in Leicester illuminate their home to celebrate Diwali

washed, groomed and decorated. Oil lamps are put around the outside of public buildings, etc. so that the darkness of the night is lit up with thousands of flames.

As Diwali is the end of the old year and the beginning of the new, it is a time of renewal. People wear new clothes and begin using new utensils and tools. Debts are paid by businessmen before the year ends, and they open new account books which are blessed on the first day of the new year. Children are lectured and told to follow the example of their elders and turn over a new leaf.

The celebrations involve giving presents, sending greetings cards, and eating specially-prepared food and sweets. As at other festivals friends and relations are visited. In the home, puja to Rama, Sita and Lakshmi takes place, devotional songs called bhajans are sung, and special dances are performed. In the temples the arti ceremony is performed.

Shivarati

The name of this festival means 'night sacred to Shiva', because worship goes on throughout the night. Compared to other festivals it is a solemn occasion marked by fasting. Some devotees of Shiva do not sleep, eat or drink for thirty-six hours.

During the night Shiva is worshipped with singing and dancing in shrines dedicated to the god. In the shrine is a linga (a small stone pillar representing the god Shiva) around which people assemble and perform puja. Offerings are made by pouring milk, honey and melted butter over the linga. When the fast ends at about four o'clock, much feasting follows with sweet potatoes and cucumbers among the many foods eaten. It is also believed that unmarried girls should keep vigil throughout the night so that Shiva can help them to find a suitable husband.

At the festival the people remember a story which helps to explain why they fast and keep a watch throughout the night. The story tells of a hunter who was once chased by a tiger. He climbed a tree to escape, and he had to perch there the whole night as the tiger crouched below. To make sure he did not fall asleep and so fall out of the tree, the hunter started plucking the leaves one by one and dropping them on the ground. There was an image of Shiva under the tree which was Shiva's favourite. As the leaves fell Shiva felt that he was being worshipped and he blessed the hunter.

Rama-navami

Rama's birthday is celebrated on this day, the ninth day of the Hindu New Year, which is in March or April. Puja to Rama takes place in the home shrines, but many people attend the temple where worship is offered to Rama, and where priests read aloud the events in Rama's life from the Ramayana. Worship also involves the singing of the Ramanama, which is the one hundred and eight names of Rama. Whenever Rama is worshipped Hanuman must be present to hear it, therefore a seat is always set aside for the monkey king. The celebrations also include processions around the neighbourhood when an image of Rama is carried round by the people.

As it is a fast day certain foods are not eaten, for instance cereals, salts and ordinary vegetables. However, on this day families do enjoy eating some of the more unusual delicacies which they cannot normally afford.

Janmashtami

This is the celebration of Krishna's birthday (Krishna is one of the incarnations of the god Vishnu, see page 76). Krishna's birth took place in prison on a dark stormy night. So many Hindus go to the temple to await the hour of his birth at midnight; when it comes they greet the baby Krishna with singing and dancing. Everyone shares sweet foods just like those given to an Indian mother shortly after her baby is born.

The following day is a fast, but in the evening there is a feast. Throughout the festivities the people listen to readings of the many stories of Krishna, and watch plays and dances describing his exploits.

Holi

This festival is held in late February or early March and lasts for five days. In India, spring is the season of love, thus Holi is sacred to Kama, the god of love, and to the great lover, Krishna. It is a celebration of the games Krishna played with the cow girls, and the beginning of his love for Radna, one of the girls. According to the legend Krishna was brought up by foster-parents in Gokula ('Cow Village') as a cowherd. As a child Krishna was a mischievous boy who often bewildered his foster mother with his tricks, so that Holi is a time for playing practical jokes.

In the celebrations puja to Krishna is performed at home, and in the temples where stories about Krishna and Radna are read and dramatized. However, much of the time during the festival is spent outside; in the streets and squares bonfires are lit and dances performed. Processions are held in which animals pull decorated carts on which are images of Krishna and Radna on swings which are adorned with flowers.

Holi is a time of real fun—red and violet powders, and coloured water are thrown over everyone in the streets. Thus it is not safe to go out in good clothes. If people return home coloured from head to foot, it is a sign that they have really enjoyed themselves!

A Holi bonfire celebration in Leicester

·Glossary·

Agni	the Indian Fire God (cf. page 87)
Ahimsa	the Hindu teaching of non-violence to all living things (cf. page 77)
Anjali	action performed in worship of placing hands together in front of the forehead (cf. page 86)
Arti	worship performed by waving lights before an image (cf. page 84)
Aryans	invaders who settled in North-west India around 1750 BC (cf. page 75)
Atman	'soul' in all conscious things; part of Brahman in all conscious beings (cf. page 76)
Avatar	form of a god that appears on earth (cf. page 76)
Benares	holy city on the banks of the River Ganges; also called Varenasi (cf. page 88)
Bhagavad-Gita	the most important part of the Hindu poem, the Mahabarata (cf. page 87)
Bhajans	hymns sung during Hindu worship (cf. page 83)
Brahma	Hindu god of creation and of all knowledge (cf. page 76)
Brahman	the Hindi name for the Supreme Eternal Being (cf. page 76)
Brahmanas	a Hindu sacred book; part of the Veda (cf. page 87)
Brahmins	members of the highest caste, i.e. priestly caste (cf. page 77)
Caste	a group in society into which a Hindu is born (cf. page 77)
Dasera	a festival day held in September/October (cf. page 89)
Diwali	a three-day or four-day festival held in October (cf. page 90)
Durga	a Hindu goddess (cf. page 89)
Durga-puja	a festival held in Bengal in September/October in honour of Durga (cf. page 89)
Epics	Hindu literature including the famous poems the Ramayana and the Mahabarata (cf. page 87)
Ganges	the Hindus' holy river which runs eastwards through North India (cf. page 88)
Gayatri Mantra	the best-known verse from the Veda; sometimes called 'the Mother of the Veda' (cf. page 85)
Ghat	steps on a river bank (cf. page 88)
Ghee	clarified butter used in worship and cooking (cf. page 86)
Guru	teacher who gives religious instruction (cf. page 79)
Hanuman	the Hindu monkey god (cf. page 87)
Harijan	'children of God'; alternative name for the outcastes or untouchables (cf. page 78)
Havan	form of worship during which fire is offered to the gods (cf. page 83)
Hindu	name given to the people who follow the dominant religion in India (cf. page 75)
Holi	festival held in February or March (cf. page 92)
Indr	warrior god to whom many hymns in the Rig-Veda are addressed (cf. page 87)
Janmashtami	festival in July or August devoted to Krishna (cf. page 91)

Karma	actions done in life which are believed to affect future life, i.e. after re-birth (cf. page 86)
Krishna	name of the best-known avatar or god of Vishnu (cf. page 76)
Kshatriya	warrior or ruling caste (cf. page 77)
Kumbha-Mela	great bathing festival held once every twelve years at the confluence of the River Ganges and the River Jumna (cf. page 89)
Lakshmi	Hindu goddess of wealth and consort of Vishnu (cf. page 90)
Laws of Manu	important Hindu law book (cf. page 87)
Linga	small stone pillar representing Shiva; used in worship (cf. page 91)
Mahabarata	an epic poem; the longest in the world (cf. page 87)
Mala	string of 108 beads used in worship (cf. page 85)
Mandale	one of the sections of the hymns found in the Rig-Veda (cf. page 87)
Mantra	sacred verse used in worship; believed to have supernatural power (cf. page 87)
Namaste	words of greeting, spoken to a person, showing respect (cf. page 86)
Navarati	festival held in September/October (cf. page 89)
Om	sacred syllable or word representing Brahman; frequently used in worship (cf. page 85)
Puja	worship of a god including the saying of prayers and the giving of offerings (cf. page 85)
Purusha	the first man from whom according to Hindu legend the castes were formed (cf. page 77)
Rama	name of an ancient king whose exploits are recorded in the Ramayana; thought of as an avatar of Vishnu (cf. page 87)
Rama-navami	festival in March/April in celebration of the life of Rama (cf. page 91)
Ravana	demon king of Sri Lanka; enemy of Rama (cf. page 87)
Reincarnation	idea that a person will be reborn on earth in another form (cf. page 77)
Rig-Veda	'Veda of Praise'; the first section of the Hindu sacred writings called the Vedic hymns (cf. page 87)
Samskaras	series of rituals undertaken by Hindus in preparation for a new phase in life (cf. page 78)
Sanskrit	ancient language in which much Hindu religious literature is written (cf. page 87)
Shiva	god of destruction and re-creation (cf. page 75)
Shivarati	festival dedicated to Shiva held in January/February (cf. page 91)
Shudras	members of the unskilled labouring and serving caste (cf. page 77)
Sita	wife of Rama (cf. page 87)
Tilaka mark	mark put on the forehead showing which god Hindus are worshipping (cf. page 85)
Upanishads	Hindu sacred writing; third section of the Veda (cf. page 87)
Vaisyas	members of the caste of skilled workers and traders (cf. page 77)
Veda	collection of ancient Hindu sacred literature; 'veda' means 'divine knowledge' (cf. page 87)
Vishnu	Hindu god; the preserver of life; god of goodness and love (cf. page 75)
Yoga	form of meditation practised by Hindus (cf. page 86)
Yogi	person who practises yoga (cf. page 86)

·Activities·

1 Important Things to Remember and Understand

Special words and ideas: ahimsa; atman; avatar; arti; caste; harijan; karma; mantra; 'om'; puja; samskaras.

2 Important Things to Find Out

Ask someone who is an expert in yoga to come and give a talk and demonstration.
Find out about famous Hindu men and women, e.g. Gandhi, and see how their lives are or were affected by their religion.
Read some of the legends of the Hindu gods, particularly those that are remembered at festival time.

3 Important Things to Discuss

What difficulties arise through observing the caste system?
Talk over the problem of a Hindu family settling in a Western country.
What do you think of Hindu attitudes to family life, marriage and death?

4 Important Things to Do

If possible, visit a Hindu temple; ask the people to allow you to see puja being performed.
Find out about Indian food; try preparing some of their dishes.

5 Written Work

a Describe a day in the life of a Hindu, particularly what religious rites and duties are carried out.
b Imagine you are taking part in some Hindu festivals; explain what happens in the celebrations and what you would do.
c What types of Hindu temple are there? Explain their important features.

CHAPTER 5

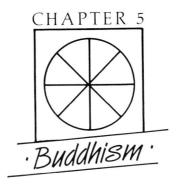

·Buddhism·

1 Beginnings

Buddhism began in India some 2500 years ago. Its founder was an Indian Hindu prince named Siddhartha Gautama, who was born in 560 BC. He became known as 'the Buddha', meaning 'the Enlightened One', after he had meditated under a fig tree and firmly believed he had found the answer to the world's suffering. He spent the rest of his life travelling around North India teaching his ideas. After his death his followers continued his work, and slowly but surely this new faith became established in Northern India.

A bronze statute of Buddha at Kamakura, Japan

The Life of the Buddha

Gautama lived in the Himalayan foothills where his father was the local ruler. He lived a life of ease and luxury in a palace, and for many years he had no contact with the unpleasant side of life, for instance, disease, poverty and suffering. When he was sixteen years old he was married to a beautiful young girl called Yasodhara, and in time they had a son. However Gautama felt uneasy about his way of living, and he thought that there was more to life as he knew it.

Gautama's life changed dramatically at the age of twenty-nine. One day he was out driving in his chariot when he saw a sight which he had never been allowed to see before. This was a group of poor suffering people: one was an old man, another a horribly diseased man, the next was lying dead, and the last was a holy man wearing a yellow robe. From experience Gautama had learned that all mankind must suffer old age, disease and death; but from the holy man he discovered that a man can release his soul from suffering. A short time later Gautama gave up his life of luxury and, leaving his wife and son, set out to find the meaning of life. He shaved his head and put on the robes of a holy man.

For the next six years Gautama wandered through Northern India seeking the answer to his problem. He spent almost two years with two famous Hindu monks, and then several years with a group of five ascetics (hermits who live a very austere life), during which time he almost starved himself to death. However none of this harsh living satisfied him. He found that the fasting only weakened his body and he could no longer think clearly. He therefore left his five companions and continued his search alone.

Eventually Gautama reached a place which is now called Bodh-Gaya, on the banks of the River Neranjara. There he sat under a fig tree in meditation for forty-six days, and achieved what Buddhists described as supreme enlightenment; that is, he believed that he had found the answer to his problem of the meaning of life. From that time on he was known as the Buddha ('the Enlightened One') or 'the One who has awakened to the truth of things'. The tree under which Gautama sat is now known as the 'Bodhi' or 'Bo' tree which means 'the tree of knowledge'.

Bodh-gaya, showing a descendant of the Bodhi-tree under which Buddha found enlightenment

Gautama was tempted to remain under the tree simply living out his life for his own sake. However he decided that this new knowledge he had gained should be passed on to others. He left Bodh-Gaya and made his way to what is called today, the Deer Park, near Benares. There he preached his first sermon in which he outlined his teaching which he called the Middle Way. This included the first statement of the Four Noble Truths and the Eightfold Path. His teaching is known as the Dharma.

His first converts were the first ascetics he had been with before his enlightenment. For the next forty-five years the Buddha (as he was now called) travelled around Northern India teaching the Middle Way. A group of disciples began to gather around him, and these in time formed a community which was called the Sangha, the Buddhist monastic order. Any man could join the Sangha by believing the Buddha's teaching and then putting it into practice. This meant that the usual rules of the Hindu caste system were not observed. After a while a similar community was established for women.

When the Buddha died in 480 BC at the age of eighty, his teaching had been widely accepted and the Sangha was firmly established. Following his death, the Buddha's body was cremated, and his remains were divided amongst his followers. These relics were placed in special stone burial mounds called stupas and they became centres of Buddhist devotion. By the time of the Emperor Asoka there were many of these stupas in India containing both the remains of the Buddha and other Buddhist saints.

The Growth of Buddhism

After the Buddha's death no leader replaced him, and little is known about the faith for the next two hundred years; but the Sangha survived and continued to follow the Buddha's teaching. However two hundred years later, in the 3rd century BC, Buddhism began to spread rapidly, mainly through the efforts of the Indian Emperor Asoka. He had become a Buddhist after being disgusted with the enormous suffering caused by war. He encouraged the spread of Buddhist teaching throughout India. He forbade the taking of human and animal life. He showed concern for the welfare of his people by providing such things as hospitals, hostels and guesthouses, new wells and plantations of trees. He put up inscriptions praising the Buddha and the Sangha. At the places of the Buddha's birth, enlightenment and death he built memorials and he encouraged Buddhists to visit them on pilgrimage. More importantly he made Buddhism much more attractive to ordinary people, and he told them particularly to visit the temples each week.

During his reign Asoka sent monks beyond the Indian boundaries on missionary journeys to spread the Buddhist faith. In time Buddhism reached Ceylon (Sri Lanka) and Indonesia in the south, and Burma, Thailand, Cambodia and Laos in the east. Not long after Asoka's death, Buddhism split into two main groups. The Southern Buddhist school or group is called Theravada which means 'the Doctrine of the Elders', (see page 106). By the 1st century AD Buddhism had also spread northwards from India into China, and then into Nepal and Tibet where it became firmly established. From China it reached Vietnam, Korea and Japan. This northern branch of Buddhism is known as the Mahayana school (see page 106), which means 'the Greater Vehicle'.

2 Initiation in Buddhism

There is no special ceremony held when a person accepts the Buddhist faith. It is sufficient to repeat sincerely the formula known as the Three Refuges, which says:

'I go to the Buddha for refuge;
I go to the Dharma for refuge;
I go to the Sangha for refuge.'

After this acceptance of the Buddha's teaching it is a matter of putting it into practice. However there is one important ceremony which is especially performed in Theravada Buddhism. This is when a young man is ordained as a monk and then enters a monastery. An important rule of the monastic order is that monks stay in the monastery to meditate and study during the rainy season (i.e. July to October). Those young men who wish to become monks must enter the monastery before this period of study begins. In fact it is the custom for most young men of twenty-one to enter the monastery at this time in order to study their religion. When the three months are past, if they wish they may return to ordinary life. On the other hand they may remain in the monastery (many parents hope that they will), but they are not obliged to make any irrevocable vows and can return to ordinary life as a layman at any time they wish.

A young man who is intending to become a monk is called a naag, and there is much activity and preparation before the actual ordination ceremony takes place. A naag must make sure that he has paid off all his debts, so that he owes no one any money. He will only be accepted as a monk if he can show that he can live a life of disciplined poverty. He makes a preliminary visit to the monastery (also called the 'wat') to make the necessary arrangements with the abbot. He learns the details of the ceremony, especially what is said. Pali, an ancient language, is used in religious ceremonies and he has to reply to questions put to him in that language.

The naag makes family visits shortly before his ordination. He calls on relations and friends who join in sponsoring him while he is in the monastery. They believe that by giving the naag such support they will gain 'merit'. On these visits the naag presents tapers, incense and flowers, and asks for a blessing. His friends also accompany him; they strike a bell or gong which shows that the young man is about to enter a monastery. On the day before the ceremony the naag processes through the streets with his friends. A large umbrella is held over his head, and he wears a white robe to show that his intentions to be a monk are pure and good. Often dancers and musicians are in the procession. It is a way of publicly showing that he intends to become a monk. The naag's parents hold a party on the same

A naag's procession

In the countries of South-east Asia, it is also usual for teenage boys to spend a month or two in a monastery as junior monks. They have their heads shaved, wear monks' robes, and live like the other monks. They always accompany the senior monks on their daily alms round.

The first Englishman to be publicly ordained a Buddhist monk

evening, and all those who attend bring presents for him. It is a very light-hearted gathering with much music and dancing.

Before the ceremony takes place the naag has to shave off all the hair on his head, including his eyebrows and beard. On the day of the ceremony he leaves home wearing elaborate rich clothing, i.e. a cone-shaped hat and a thin net robe embroidered in gold. These clothes represent those worn by Gautama before he gave up his life of luxury as a prince. The young man reverently makes his way to the wat holding a wax candle, a joss stick and a flower between his palms. He walks round the wat four times, then removes his princely robe and throws coins to the crowds. Next his father takes him to the ordination hall where the monks and the elders are seated waiting for his arrival. He approaches the monks (called 'bhikkhus'), then he sits down on his heels before them holding in his arms the yellow monk's robes he will wear. He then asks in Pali for his ordination; when the monks agree he leaves briefly to put on his monk's robes. When he returns he asks the abbot to instruct him. The abbot describes a monk's life and asks the naag a few questions. If the answers are satisfactory, and none of the monks object, the young man is admitted to the Sangha and his religious training begins.

The Life of the Monk

All monks must observe ten rules (commandments) which guide them in their everyday living. The first five of these are rules known as the 'Five Precepts' and also apply to all other Buddhists. The remaining rules apply only to monks. The rules are:

1 They must not take the life of any living creature.

2 They must not steal anyone's possessions.

3 They must not be involved in sexual misconduct.

4 They must not tell any lies.

5 They must not use any alcohol or misuse drugs.

6 They must not eat after midday.

7 They must not attend shows where there is music or dancing.

8 They must not use any perfumes or personal jewellery.

9 They must not sleep on raised or upholstered beds.

10 They must not accept gifts of gold or silver.

A Buddhist monk has very few possessions. Besides his robe he has a begging bowl for food, a razor for shaving and a filter to strain insects from his drinking water. He lives in a small hut in the monastery which is very simply furnished. Every morning soon after daybreak he goes on his alms round. He regularly visits the same households each day in the neighbourhood of the monastery to receive a contribution of food which is placed in his begging bowl. Each household willingly gives the food as it is part of a Buddhist's religious duty to support the monks. He then returns to the monastery to eat his meal, and follows this with a period of worship and meditation. For the remainder of the morning he follows some useful activity, e.g. studying or teaching the local children. Shortly before noon he eats the last meal of the day. From that time he must fast, but he is allowed to drink water or tea without milk or sugar. He occupies himself throughout the afternoon and evening with further study and meditation. At some point there will be communal devotions in which all the monks participate. Also the monk may meet and talk to lay people who visit the monastery, and he may take a walk in the neighbourhood during the cooler hours of the evening.

Buddhist monks in a temple at Bangkok

Other Ceremonies in Buddhism
Marriage

In Buddhism as in some other major religions people generally leave it to their parents to choose a suitable marriage partner for them. There is no religious wedding ceremony in the temple or monastery; instead a simple ceremony takes place in the home. The bride and groom exchange vows promising to honour and respect each other. Also present are a group of girls, wearing white costumes (which symbolize 'purity'), who recite devotional verses. A monk may attend some ceremonies. He ties the thumbs of the groom to those of the bride with a piece of thread as a symbol of their unity. Later on the bride and groom visit the monastery to receive the blessing of the monks and to hear a sermon on the Buddha's teaching about married life.

Burmese monks setting off on their alms round

Funerals

When a member of a family dies the relatives and other mourners are reminded of the impermanence of life. The relatives invite the monks from the monastery to the house or to the cemetery for the funeral. The body of the dead person is placed in a coffin and then taken in procession for burial. Buddhists may be buried or cremated. At the graveside the monks recite the Three Refuges and the Five Precepts (see pp 98/9). The relatives also perform two symbolic actions. The white cloth which covered the coffin is given to the monks who are asked to share the merit they have gained with the person who has died. The other action is to pour water into a cup until it overflows; this represents the transfer of merit to the deceased person. The monks then recite suitable verses and give a sermon about life and death.

At fixed intervals after the funeral, usually seven days, three months and one year, the bereaved give meals to the monks, and it is believed the merit resulting from such actions is passed on to the person who has died.

3 Buddhist Holy Buildings

Monasteries

The main centres of Buddhist life are the monasteries. These are not closed communities simply for the monks. The monasteries are built and provided by the ordinary Buddhist lay people who take an active interest in the Sangha by visiting the community regularly for both worship and study.

The monastery itself consists of a number of buildings covering a sizeable area which is surrounded by a wall. In the monastery grounds are trees and shrubs with well-tended sanded spaces where both monks and lay people walk and rest.

The buildings in the monastery enclosure are of varying size and importance. There are small simply furnished houses in which the monks live. They contain a mat used as a bed, a water jar, a stand for the monk's begging bowl, a small shrine for daily devotions, and perhaps a few books. The monks and lay people assemble at regular intervals on holy days in a large hall to hear sermons and lectures on Buddhist teaching and beliefs.

The most important and often the most beautiful building is the shrine which is always built facing east. It always contains a large figure of the Buddha, usually in the seated position. Regular devotions, the ordination of monks and the regular recitation of the monastic law are held there. Usually there is a pagoda which contains a relic of some Buddhist holy man or even of the Buddha himself. As the people may not enter these buildings, in front of them there may be a small shrine containing images of the Buddha where people may sit and meditate.

At many of the large monasteries there is usually a Bo or fig tree growing. These trees are revered because the Buddha sat under such a tree when he became enlightened, and because they remind the Buddhists of their goal in life. Also many monasteries contain a building which serves as a school which the local children attend in order to learn reading and writing.

A pagoda, Japan

Buddhist Shrines and Temples

These are the main places of worship. They may be built within a monastery enclosure or in a particular holy place, e.g. at Bodh-Gaya where the Buddha received enlightenment. There is a Bo Tree at Bodh-Gaya which is said to be a descendant of the one under which the Buddha sat.

Buddhist temples and shrines are built to symbolize the Five Elements of the faith, i.e. earth, fire, air, water and wisdom. Each element has a symbol so that when they are arranged in the correct order, they outline the general shape of a temple or shrine. These symbols are arranged vertically beginning from the base with a square (earth), followed by an oval (air), a circle (fire), a horizontal line (water), and finally a vertical line (wisdom). Thus all Buddhist holy buildings have a broad base (symbolizing 'earth') with a spire or point at the top (symbolizing 'wisdom').

The most important feature of the temple is the shrine room. Here there is always a statue of the Buddha in the seated position of meditation. There are always flowers, incense sticks and candles around the statue, and near its foot places to put offerings.

Before the statue there is an open space where the people sit for worship and meditation, and a preacher's stand from which readings are given.

Temples and shrines are not simply places of worship. They are centres of Buddhist social life. Buddhist people spend much of their surplus money on their temples and shrines with the result that these buildings are the finest in the community, being magnificent examples of religious architecture, and containing much wonderful painting and sculpture.

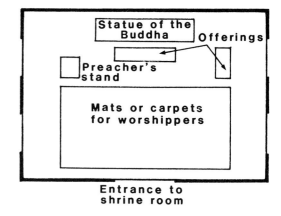

A plan of a shrine room in a Buddhist temple or monastery

Pilgrimage to Buddhist Shrines and Temples

In the Buddhist religion there are a number of places which have become centres of pilgrimage. Buddhists like to visit them in order to carry out acts of worship. There are no particular rituals which have to be observed; it is sufficient simply to have worshipped there. Many of these places of pilgrimage are closely associated with the life of the Buddha in some way, e.g. at Bodh-Gaya where he sat under the Bo Tree and was enlightened. Also when Buddha died he was cremated, and some of his remains (now called relics) were sent to various Buddhist centres, where shrines were built to house them. One of the most famous is the Temple of the Sacred Tooth at Kandy in Sri Lanka because it contains one of the Buddha's teeth set in silver.

A Buddhist temple in Kathmandu

4 Buddhist Worship

There is no particular day of the week for worship; generally their holy days are governed by the phases of the moon. Buddhists have always gathered together in their temples to meditate and to venerate the Buddha in the shrine room.

In the Shrine

Before entering, the people remove their shoes, then go and sit on mats facing the image of Buddha. Worship is silent as, in general, people meditate on the Buddha's teaching and example. As they worship, they perform the anjali, i.e. they place the palms of their hands together before their forehead and then stretch them up towards the Buddha's image. Next they will prostrate three times in honour of the Buddha, the Dharma and the Sangha. The offerings of flowers and of light (by lighting candles) are made.

There are usually monks present as well, and at intervals they repeat Buddhist chants. As certain phrases are spoken all the

Worshippers in the shrine room

people prostrate before the Buddha's image. One of the monks sits on the preacher's stand and reads aloud from the Buddhist scriptures, and at a convenient time a sermon is given by a monk. Shortly afterwards the monks leave, and the people remain to drink tea and chat together; thus worship ends with a social gathering.

Individual Worship

Buddhist people also worship on their own each day. This may be carried out in the Temple shrine or in the shrine at home. This devotion is very simple in form; it consists of kneeling before the image of the Buddha, offering flowers, money or food, and lighting a candle. Then they pray and meditate. Some people only repeat texts from the Buddhist scriptures, as the Buddha taught that prayer was useless because there is no 'One' to whom to pray. However many people appear to pray to the Buddha and his Bodhisattvas (see page 106) to ask for guidance and help in time of trouble.

Meditation

Since meditation is so important in the Buddhist faith, most Buddhists meditate each day. Some put an hour or two aside each day for this purpose. The Buddha himself demonstrated the importance of meditation since he presented a clear outline of it in the last three stages of the Eightfold Path, i.e. right effort, right mindfulness and right concentration (see page 105). Buddhists are taught that the purpose of meditation is to help them achieve enlightenment or, to put it another way, it is a practical way of reaching Nirvana (see page 104).

In meditation Buddhists develop the mind to heights beyond normal understanding. By continual practice they can cut themselves off from the world around. They achieve a state of mind where all confused thoughts are stilled, and as a result they are able to rise to a higher place of existence, free from thought, pain, worry and all the problems of life. It is like passing beyond the world to a place of perfect peace. After meditating they feel like new creatures, mentally alert and self-controlled, and better able to cope with all the stress and problems of everyday living.

When performing meditation Buddhists may bow, kneel or even prostrate before the image of Buddha. Usually they sit perfectly still on the floor (sometimes adopting the same position the Buddha used when he meditated under the fig tree). They think about their lives, confess wrong-doing, and generally try to clear the mind of all unnecessary thought. They repeat quietly sacred texts from the holy books. They may use some of the topics which have been set down to be used in meditation, e.g. the Buddha and his qualities, the Dharma, the Sangha and its qualities, and loving kindness.

5 Buddhist Beliefs

In Hindu doctrine there are two important ideas that have passed over into Buddhism; these are samsara and karma. Samsara means 'continuation' or 'carrying on'. Buddhists say that men are reborn into a new life when they die. Life, for Buddhists, is an endless round of existences, i.e. being born, dying and being reborn. This is called the Samsara cycle, and in order to escape from the constant round of birth and rebirth, a Buddhist seeks to reach Nirvana. The force that keeps the endless round of existences continuing is called karma. Indian people believe that everything a person does creates a kind of force which is carried forward into the next life when he is reborn. If a bad life has been lived, then he will be reborn in a lower station in the next life. Buddhists believe that the only way to avoid being reborn is to achieve a state of mind where this force of karma no longer affects them. This state of mind is the Buddhist's goal and it is what they call Nirvana.

The main Buddhist beliefs may be divided into three main parts, i.e. the Three Universal Truths, the Four Noble Truths and the Eightfold Path. In his first public sermon in the Deer Park following his enlightenment the Buddha outlined his religious ideas and explained the basic principles. These are found in the Four Noble Truths and the Eightfold Path.

The Three Universal Truths
These basic Buddhist ideas are known by the terms anicca, dukkha and anatta.

1 Anicca means 'impermanence'; the Buddha taught that nothing is the same from one moment to the next, e.g. people change physically every minute, and so life is in a state of change. Therefore there is no rest in this world, and everything men possess which makes them what they are, is subject to change.
2 The second truth is dukkha meaning 'suffering'. This covers many things, e.g. pain, disease, boredom, discomfort, etc., and there is no way of avoiding suffering. The Buddha's teaching seeks to overcome this problem; his answer is to use wisdom. By this he means the ability to see into the true nature of things so that, by using this wisdom, Nirvana is eventually reached.
3 Anatta or 'no soul' is the third idea. The Buddha taught that man does not have a soul. He said there is nothing more to a man than can be seen or experienced, and that man is made up of five things: the body, feeling, ideas, mental actions and awareness. The Buddha's ideas are not at all clear on this subject; in fact they conflict with the Hindu teaching on reincarnation, which says that part of man carries over into the next life. Some Buddhists have taught that energy is created by all people and it is this that carries on into the next life.

The Four Noble Truths
These are a central part of the Buddha's

teaching. He explained that if the Truths are understood and then accepted the way to new life is open to all.

1 The first of the Truths says that all life involves dukkha, i.e. suffering. (You will remember that this was also the second of the Three Universal Truths.)

2 The second explains that all men suffer because of desire, i.e. they desire to cling on to the cycle of birth, death and rebirth in spite of the suffering involved.

3 The third Truth declares that only by crushing desire can men avoid suffering.

4 The fourth Truth says that there is a way of escaping from suffering in this world and so entering Nirvana. The way of escape is by means of the Eightfold Path which the Buddha described as the Middle Way between two ways of life: between, on the one hand, the very strict life of self-discipline which many Hindu holy men practised; and, on the other, the overindulgent life of luxury and ease of rich people.

— The Four Noble Truths —

1. *Suffering is part of life.*
2. *Suffering is due to selfish desires.*
3. *Suffering will stop if these desires are crushed.*
4. *The way to crush desire is to follow the eight fold path.*

The Four Noble Truths

The Eightfold Path

There are three stages to be followed in the Eightfold Path. The first two steps are taken as a result of being enlightened, and consist of making a definite decision to follow the Path. The next three steps show how a Buddhist must behave after taking the decision, and the last three deal with spiritual training, or meditation whereby a Buddhist learns to achieve the state of mind to enter Nirvana.

The eight steps in the Buddhist way of life are:

Right Belief:	this is to accept the Buddha's teaching as the necessary means to enter Nirvana.
Right Resolve:	to carry out the Buddha's teaching by following the Eightfold Path.
Right Speech:	to speak no unkind or harsh words, and not to tell lies.
Right Action:	to keep the commandments which forbid a person to do any harm to any living thing; for instance, not to take life, to steal, to commit adultery, or to take alcohol or drugs.
Right Livelihood:	to follow an occupation which fits in with the Buddha's teaching, and which is useful and helpful.
Right Effort:	by living life correctly it is easier to control and develop the mind so that the aim of ridding oneself of all evil and seeking only the good is more easily achieved.
Right Mindfulness:	to control the mind carefully when practising contemplation and meditation.

Right Concentration: to be able to meditate with the correct concentration and thus train the mind to the point where a person is ready to enter Nirvana.

These eight steps of the Buddhist Way are symbolized by the eight spokes of the Buddhist Wheel of Life shown at the start of the Chapter and in more detail here.

These teachings are found in all branches of Buddhism, but with the development of the two main groups in the Buddhist faith, i.e. Theravada and Mahayana, different ideas were introduced. These ideas are only accepted by the members of those particular groups.

Theravada Buddhism

The followers of Theravada Buddhism believe that they have kept to the original teaching of the Buddha and say that they have not adopted any of the beliefs of the countries into which Buddhist ideas spread. For this reason they use the name 'Theravada', which means 'Doctrine of the Elders'. Theravada Buddhists regard the Buddha as a human being, but say that he is a great man for all to follow. They also say that the Buddha, or anyone else, can only save mankind by showing the way to live.

For them, the ideal person is the arahat—one who follows the Buddha's teaching as described in the Middle Way, and the ideal life is that of a homeless monk. In practice this means that not everyone can receive salvation, since it is not possible for everyone to live a life of self-denial and homelessness. Salvation is not offered to all. This branch of Buddhism is also called Hinayana or the Lesser Vehicle.

Mahayana Buddhism

Mahayana Buddhism is also known as the Northern way or the Greater Vehicle, and its distinctive ideas concern the person of the Buddha himself. They say that the Buddha was more than a human being. He was in fact an Eternal Being who had appeared on earth in human form at different times, and Gautama the Buddha was the fourth appearance of this Being. Because of this, some Mahayana Buddhists worship the Buddha as a kind of god. They also believe in ideal people called Bodhisattvas: these are holy people whom they say have already gained Nirvana, but out of compassion for others, they remain in the world to help them along the path to Nirvana. Therefore they are thought of as saviours and ordinary Buddhist people worship them. To the Mahayana Buddhists Nirvana is a heavenly place which can be entered through faith in the Buddha.

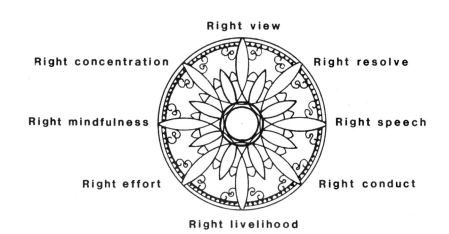

The Eightfold Path

6 Buddhist Sacred Writings

Buddhist teachings, like those of many religions, were passed on orally at first, however, within a short time, some monks began to make written records of it. Eventually a council was held at Rajgir in order to produce an agreed version of the Buddha's teaching. The existing versions of the Buddha's teaching were read aloud to an assembly of five hundred monks, and each section was checked by Ananda, a cousin of the Buddha, and Upali, a learned monk. A final version was then agreed and to show that it was accepted as a true record it was chanted aloud in unison by 500 monks.

There are no remains of the texts of this teaching in existence today. The earliest fragments of the Buddha's teaching are carved as inscriptions on stone monuments which were set up on the orders of the Emperor Asoka round about 250 BC. The oldest complete manuscript is a copy of the Way of Virtue (a Theravada Buddhist book), written on birch-bark in the 2nd century AD. In time the teaching was put into books by the two main branches of Buddhism so that each now has its own sacred books.

The Theravada Books

The Theravada Buddhists call their books Tri-pitake (meaning 'three baskets'). They say they are containers of the Buddha's teaching and are written in Pali.

1 The first 'basket' is Discipline, and it consists mainly of the rules of living for the monks.
2 The second 'basket' is the teaching of the Buddha.
3 The third 'basket', called 'Near Teaching', contains long explanations, commentary and development of the teaching.

The second basket, 'The Teaching', is by far the most important. It contains the doctrines of the Buddha and his followers, and 547 stories of the Buddha (including some of his previous lives), and of other Buddhas before him. One important story is an account of the Buddha's final descent from heaven to become a Buddha and to bring his teaching to the world. There are also psalms written by monks and nuns. Perhaps the most important section is 'The Path of Virtue', containing 423 verses, which most

The Diamond Scripture

Buddhists can recite by heart. It records the first sermon of the Buddha which he made in the Deer Park at Benares.

The Mahayana Buddhists
Their sacred writings include the Tri-pitake, but they also use other writings called the Sutras, which are written in Sanskrit, the language of the Hindu scriptures. The most important are the Diamond Scripture and the Lotus Scripture or the Lotus of Wonderful Law. The lotus is a symbol of the Buddha and his teaching. The lotus flower germinates under water then floats to the surface to open out. So the Buddha is born in an imperfect world but rises above it through enlightenment.

The Lotus Scripture includes the description of the Buddha appearing on a mountain peak in the Himalayas surrounded by thousands of arahats, Bodhisattvas and gods. He announces that the life followed by monks is too narrow since only a few people are saved. He declares that there will be a broad way of salvation for all mankind, a way of faith and grace so that all who call upon him by faith will be saved. The book also introduces the idea of Bodhisattvas (i.e. 'Buddhas-to-be') who have turned from entering Nirvana to return to the world to help others on the road to salvation.

The Use of the Books in Worship
All Buddhists use their books in worship and meditation. They quietly chant many of the passages, especially the Three Refuges. Monks also read passages aloud when they assemble for worship in the temples and shrines. In the monasteries the monks study the scriptures constantly and during their corporate worship, passages are read aloud by a monk to the other assembled monks.

7 Zen Buddhism

'Zen' is the Japanese translation of the Chinese word 'Chan' meaning 'meditation'. This branch of Buddhism is believed to have originated with the Buddha's golden lotus sermon. The Buddha took hold of the flower, held it up without speaking and then smiled. Only one disciple, Mahakasyapa, saw the point, and since then his insight has passed down through many generations. It eventually reached China in AD 552 through the Buddhist teacher, Bodhidharma. It became the most important school of Buddhism in China. From there it spread to Japan where it was soon firmly established.

The Aim of Zen Buddhism
The aim is to achieve enlightenment, which Japanese Buddhists call 'satori'. This state cannot be described or explained. No one knows what it is until he has attained it as it is an 'awareness'. This awareness is said to be transmitted from mind to mind like a flame passed from candle to candle. Satori may come as a sudden vision or as a slow awakening. It brings a sense of certainty, of tranquillity, of 'being at one' with all things. A Buddhist who achieves enlightenment becomes a new person, and for the first time fully experiences the nature of his own person and of the Universe. This is more than knowing about things: knowing in this sense means a person must go beyond rational thought to intuitive thinking.

The Zen Method of Thinking and Meditation
One way used by Zen teachers to bring their pupils to the advanced level of thought is to give them endless unsolvable problems called koans. The idea is to pass beyond the limits of rational thinking so that sudden illumination is achieved. Examples of koans are 'How many elephants are there in a blade of grass?' and 'What is the sound of one hand clapping?' These koans are nonsense; they deliberately baffle people's minds and force them to the limits of reasoned thinking to the point where intuitive knowledge is achieved. ('Intuitive knowledge' is knowledge gained by suddenly realizing the answer to a problem.)

Generally a Zen novice monk offers his thoughts on a particular koan to his teacher who knows immediately if he has the point; if not he is told to go away and think again. The Zen method also includes hitting the novice and throwing him to the floor. It is thought a sudden blow can help the novice to break through the limits of reasoned thinking, and in this way save years of meditation.

Monks in Zen Buddhism
The monks have very active lives running the monastery and working in the fields. Meditation is the main activity. This is called zazen and it is carried out sitting cross-legged overlooking a garden of rocks and raked sand, and involves strict breathing control. Zen monasteries usually have seven buildings, including the main meditation hall and the lecture hall, where the monks and other Zen followers meet to hear readings of the Buddha's sutras.

The Influence of Zen Buddhism
Chinese art has been greatly influenced by Zen Buddhism. Its teaching that man and nature are one has inspired paintings of nature which show sensitivity and a great sense of space. In Japanese art simplicity is everything. A few lines of paint or a single spray of flowers can say all that is necessary.

The famous Japanese tea ceremony also expresses the Zen idea. The ceremonial preparation and drinking of the tea aims to

A Zen garden of rocks, moss and raked sand in Kyoto

bring about a mood which leads to peace and enlightenment. It was devised by Japanese warriors who transformed an ordinary everyday activity into a sacrament where even the simplest actions are important. The ceremony grew out of a ritual performed by Zen monks who successively drank out of a bowl before an image of Bodhidharma (see page 108).

8 Buddhist Festivals and Celebration

Both the Theravada and Mahayana branches of Buddhism have important times of celebration during the year. Many of these are associated with the life of the Buddha and with the veneration of his relics as well as the relics of other holy men.

Theravada Buddhism

Magha Puja
On the full moon in February a celebration is held to remember the time when the Buddha laid down the rules for Buddhist monks and when he ordained 1250 monks, who had been enlightened, and then addressed them on his teachings. The temples at this time are lit with 1250 candles.

New Year
The New Year is celebrated in various ways in different countries. In Sri Lanka it is mainly a water festival. There are parades of

decorated carts and floats through the streets. In the shrines the images of the Buddha are ceremonially bathed, the monks are entertained and presented with gifts. It is a light-hearted occasion; much water is thrown around on relatives, friends and strangers, and water fights are organized. The same thing happens in Laos and Cambodia, when processions of monks and young men take place. In the pagodas special honour is given to the Buddha after which national dances are performed. In Thailand it is a time for showing special regard for birds and fish. The people buy birds in cages with the intention of releasing them during the festival. Also people catch fish which have been stranded in pools when ponds and canals begin to dry up, as New Year is held during the dry season. The fish are kept in jars and released in rivers on New Year's Day. It is believed that releasing these creatures in this way is a means of gaining merit.

Wesak

This is the most important festival in the Buddhist calendar. It takes place at full moon in May and lasts for three days during which the birth, enlightenment, and the death of the Buddha are commemorated. Gifts are exchanged, houses decorated with candles, lanterns and garlands of flowers, and magnificent processions are held in the streets.

The Buddhist people gather in the shrine rooms either in the temples or in their own homes. The shrines are beautifully decorated with flowers and special offerings are placed at the foot of the image of the Buddha. Monks give talks about the Buddha's enlightenment, and about the teachings on his sufferings and on the Eightfold Path. The Buddha is specially praised for his compassion and, as a symbol of this, captive birds are set free. In the eastern countries of the world gifts of food and money are secretly left on the doorsteps of poor people, but in other parts of the world Buddhists give one-twentieth of their earnings to charity.

Poson

This celebration is held in Sri Lanka on the day of the full moon in June, particularly at the town of Mihintale. It was here that the Buddhist faith was first brought to the island, and it therefore marks the beginning of Buddhism in Sri Lanka. The people remember the arrival of Mahinda, the son of the Emperor Asoka, who had sent him to bear the message of Buddhism to the island during the 3rd century BC.

Asala

This is another festival which takes place on full moon day. On this occasion it is in July and commemorates three events in the life of the Buddha, i.e. the time of his conception, his decision to leave his life of luxury and become a monk, and his first sermon in the Deer Park near Benares.

Perahera

Kandy in Sri Lanka is the main centre for the celebration of this festival which lasts for ten days in August. On each night up to the new moon a procession makes its way through the streets. The procession contains gaily decorated elephants, drummers, dancers and torch-bearers. The elephants carry on their backs caskets containing the relics of famous Buddhist men which are normally kept in the Temple of the Sacred Tooth. (Usually only a replica of the Tooth casket is used). This festival is a great tourist attraction, but many Buddhists consider a visit to Kandy as a pilgrimage since it is thought attendance at festival time brings great merit.

Mahayana Buddhism

Oban

In July the festival of Oban is celebrated by Japanese Buddhists. It is a time of remembering family ancestors. Their spirits are guided back to their homes for their annual visit by twenty-seven lighted lanterns. After the spirits have been given offerings of food the festival comes to an end with displays of folk dancing.

The annual festival of Perahera in Kandy

'Lost Souls' or 'All Souls Day'

This Chinese Buddhist festival is similar to Oban. In September the people aim to help the souls of those departed who have no descendants to care for them. Offerings are made for lost souls, lanterns made from lotus leaves are carried, and lighted candles are placed in paper boats to honour these lost souls. This last practice refers in particular to the belief that the souls of drowned people have no resting place. In the temple a large paper boat is ceremonially burned to help the souls across the sea of torment to reach Nirvana. The celebrations in this festival show how the Buddhists in China have taken into their faith some ancient beliefs from the traditional Chinese worship of ancestors.

Higan

In Japan prayers are also offered on behalf of the dead at the Higan festival which is held twice a year, in the spring and in the autumn. Prayers and gifts for the dead are offered, although some Buddhists say it is sufficient to offer thanks for the lives of the departed and listen to sermons given in the monasteries.

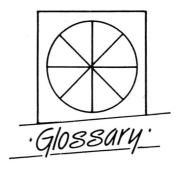

·Glossary·

Anatta	means 'no soul'; the Buddhist teaching that man has no soul (cf. page 104)
Anicca	means 'impermanence'; the Buddhist idea that all life is in a continuous state of change (cf. page 104)
Anjali	see Hindu glossary
Arahat	'the ideal person'; one who follows the Buddha's teaching as described in the Middle Way (cf. page 106)
Asala	festival held in July commemorating events in the Buddha's life (cf. page 110)
Asoka	the Indian Emperor who lived in the 3rd century BC and who became a Buddhist (cf. page 97)
Bhikku	a Buddhist monk (cf. page 99)
Bodh-Gaya	place where the Buddha became enlightened (cf. page 97)
Bodhisattva	a person who had achieved enlightenment but who remains in the world to help others achieve Nirvana (cf. page 106)
Buddha	the title given to Gautama following his enlightenment (cf. page 97)
Dharma	name given to the Buddha's teaching as outlined in the Four Noble Truths and the Eightfold Path (cf. page 97)
Dukkha	means 'suffering'; the Buddhist teaching that suffering is an inevitable part of living (cf. page 104)
Five Precepts	the Five Rules accepted by all Buddhists (cf. page 99)
Gautama	see **Siddhartha Gautama**
Higan	Japanese Buddhist festival held in spring and autumn (cf. page 111)
Hinayana	means 'Lesser Vehicle'; alternative name for Theravada Buddhism (cf. page 106)
Karma	see Hindu glossary
Koans	unsolvable problems given to novice monks in Zen Buddhism (cf. page 108)
Magha Puja	festival held in February commemorating the rule of Buddhist monks (cf. page 109)
Mahayana	means 'Greater Vehicle'; the name of the Northern branch of Buddhism (cf. page 106)
Naag	name given to a young man about to be ordained as a monk (cf. page 98)
Nirvana	the goal of all Buddhists; to achieve a state of mind such that they will not be reborn and live again in another body on earth (cf. page 104)
Oban	festival celebrated by Japanese Buddhists in July (cf. page 110)
Pagoda	Buddhist holy building, often containing a holy relic (cf. page 101)
Pali	ancient language used in Buddhist ceremonies (cf. page 98)
Poson	Buddhist celebration held in Sri Lanka in June (cf. page 110)
Samsara	means 'continuation', 'carrying on'; the endless cycle of existences experienced by people until Nirvana is reached (cf. page 104)

Sangha	the community of Buddhist monks (cf. page 97)
Satori	word for 'enlightenment' used by Japanese Buddhists (cf. page 108)
Siddhartha Gautama	the full name of the Buddha before he was enlightened (cf. page 96)
Stupa	stone burial mound containing a relic of the Buddha and other Buddhist holy men (cf. page 97)
Sutras	holy writings of the Mahayana Buddhists (cf. page 108)
Theravada	Southern branch of Buddhism; also called Hinayana; means 'Lesser Vehicle' (cf. page 106)
Three Refuges	sacred formula spoken regularly by Buddhists in meditation (cf. page 98)
Tri-pitake	sacred writings of the Theravada Buddhists (cf. page 107)
Wat	Buddhist monastery (cf. page 98)
Wesak	the most important festival in the Buddhist calendar; held in May; celebrates the main events in the Buddha's life (cf. page 110)
Yasodhara	the wife of Gautama (cf. page 96)
Zazen	type of meditation used by Zen Buddhists (cf. page 109)
Zen	means 'meditation'; the name of Japanese Buddhism (cf. page 108)

· Activities ·

1 Important Things to Remember and Understand

Special words and ideas: arahat; anicca; Bodhisattva; dharma; dukkha; Nirvana; samsara; reincarnation.

2 Important Things to Find Out

If possible, talk to people who have become Buddhists and find out how their new faith has changed their lives.
Study the lifestyle of the people in a Buddhist country to discover how religion affects daily living.
Find out what forms of meditation Buddhists use.

3 Important Things to Discuss

Is it possible for a Buddhist to fight in a war?
Why are many young people attracted to the Buddhist faith?
What can people living in the Western world learn from the Buddhist faith?

4 Important Things to Do

Make a chart of Buddhist beliefs using the Wheel of Life symbol as the centrepiece.
Draw a map of Asia; mark the main Buddhist centres and illustrate with an appropriate picture.
Make a poster of the various types of Buddhist temple and indicate their country of origin.

5 Written Work:

a Describe the life of a Buddhist monk. How does it differ from the life of an ordinary Buddhist?
b Imagine you were present when Gautama the Buddha gave his first sermon in the Deer Park. Explain what he said and what his listeners thought.
c Explain what are, in practice, the main differences between Theravada and Mahayana Buddhism.

CHAPTER 6

·Sikhism·

1 The Beginnings of Sikhism

The centre of the Sikh religion is the Punjab, a region in the north-west of the Indian subcontinent. The name 'Punjab' means 'five streams'; these are five rivers which rise in the Himalayan Mountains and flow into the River Indus. To the north of the Punjab are the foothills of the Himalayas, to the west the mountains of the North-west Frontier along the border of Pakistan and Afghanistan, and the Thar Desert is to the south and east. The land is very fertile but it has to be irrigated, otherwise the crops will not grow. In the past the Punjab was thought of as the granary of India.

It was in the Punjab that the founder of the Sikh religion lived and worked during the late 15th and early 16th centuries. He was an Indian guru or teacher named Nanak. At this time the Punjab was part of the Muslim Mogul Empire which controlled North-west India until the beginning of the 18th century. Akbar (1556–1605), one of the more tolerant Muslim rulers, gave the Sikhs the land on which Amritsar, their holy city, is built.

Nanak was greatly influenced by the Hindus and the Muslims, and many of his ideas were taken from these two religions. He was particularly influenced by Kabir (1440–1518), a Hindu teacher who originally had been born into a Muslim family. Kabir taught that there was only one God, and through devotion to Him Hindus could find release from the Law of Karma, and from the endless cycle of birth and re-birth. He also said that there were too

many rituals, ceremonies and pilgrimages; living a good life in devotion to God was more important.

During his lifetime Nanak had many followers and shortly before his death he appointed his successor from amongst these disciples. This man became the new guru. There were ten gurus in succession, the last dying in 1708. By this time Sikhism was an independent religion with its own distinctive beliefs and practices.

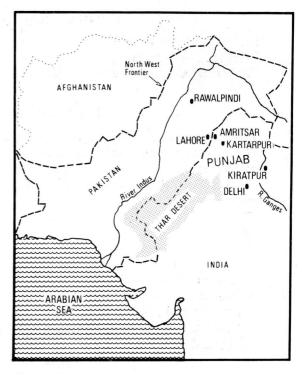

The Punjab

2 The Ten Gurus

For over 200 years the Sikhs were led by a series of gurus. Before a guru died he usually indicated who was to succeed him. In this way ten gurus led the Sikhs until the death of the tenth one. Each guru believed that through him Nanak continued to reveal the truth of God. They always used Nanak's name when teaching their followers, as Sikh doctrine is based on what Nanak taught.

The First Guru: Nanak 1469–1534
He was born near Lahore in a village which is now called Nankana Sahib. He was of a high caste and well-educated but when he was a young man he refused to accept Hindu religious duties. He married a girl from the same caste and they had several children. However he was always interested in religion, so at the age of thirty, after unsuccessfully working in commerce and agriculture, he became a wandering teacher.

Guru Nanak

He wrote a poem called the Japji, describing the nature of God, which is the basis of his teaching. He taught his followers to believe in one God, and that living a harsh solitary life (like some Hindus) was to be avoided.

Eventually he settled at Kartarpur where he founded a community of disciples called Sikhs (the word 'Sikh' means 'one who learns'). One important feature of this community was that it had a communal kitchen where free food was served to all who came regardless of caste or belief. Shortly before he died in 1534 Nanak appointed Lehna as his successor; he was known as Guru Angad.

The Second Guru; Angad 1504–1552
Angad began the work of putting together the writings that make up the Sikh holy book, the Granth. He also devised a written form of Punjabi, the Sikh language, which he called gurmukhi. As very few Sikhs could read he started providing education for young children. Angad also started building Sikh temples called gurdwaras where the Sikhs worshipped and where Sikh beliefs were taught.

The Third Guru: Amar Das 1479–1574
His most important contribution was to stress Nanak's teaching on caste and on the idea that all Sikhs should eat together. This meant in practice that one of the main rules of the Hindu caste system should not be observed. Amar Das also made the langar (communal kitchen) an important feature of the gurdwara. It was decided that all Sikhs should serve in the langar, and everyone should sit together and eat the same food including all visitors, whether rich or poor, and even the gurus themselves.

The Fourth Guru: Ram Das 1534–1581
He was responsible for making Amritsar the centre of the Sikh faith. The Mogul Emperor, Akbar, had given some land to the wife of Ram Das. On this land a city (later called

The entrance to the causeway leading to the Golden Temple

Amritsar) was established and it soon became a thriving community. Ram Das also began the building of the Golden Temple there. He ordered a large tank (pool) to be constructed with an island in the middle; on the island the temple was later built.

The Fifth Guru: Arjun Dev 1563–1606
Under the guidance of Arjun Dev the Sikh faith became established more firmly than ever in North India. The building of the Golden Temple was begun in 1589 and it was soon completed. He also completed the compilation of the Sikh holy book, the Granth, which had been started by Angad, the second guru.

In 1606 Arjun Dev was imprisoned by the Mogul Emperor, Jehangir, who falsely accused him of aiding some rebels. Eventually he was tortured to death. Before he died he appointed his son, Har Gobind, as his successor, and he instructed him to train a Sikh army to defend their faith when necessary.

The Sixth Guru: Har Gobind 1595–1644
He organized the Sikhs into an efficient army. In 1627 when Shah Jehar became the Mogul Emperor, war broke out between the Sikhs and their Muslim rulers. The Sikhs made Kiratpur in the Himalayan foothills their headquarters, and generally they used guerrilla tactics. The Sikhs were superb soldiers, but usually they only fought if they were attacked. Before he died Har Gobind indicated that his grandson, Har Rai, should succeed him.

The Seventh Guru: Har Rai 1630–1661
He was a peaceful man who did not become involved in politics. He tried without success to make peace with the Mogul Emperors. Before he died Har Rai said that Hari Krishen (his young son aged five) should succeed him.

The Eighth Guru: Hari Krishen 1656–1664
His rule as guru did not last very long. The

Mogul Emperor, Aurangzeb, wanted to replace Hari Krishen as guru, so he ordered him to come to Delhi. Once there he contracted smallpox and died. However, before his death, Hari Krishen declared that the next guru would be found in Bahala. This turned out to be Teg Bahadur, another son of Har Rai, the seventh guru.

The Ninth Guru: Teg Bahadur 1621–1675
Teg Bahadur was not accepted at first by all the Sikhs as the guru, so he left the Punjab and went to Patna where his son, Gobind Rai, was born. As the Sikhs were being increasingly persecuted by the Muslims, some Sikh leaders begged Teg Bahadur to return. He agreed and began travelling around the Punjab urging the Sikhs to stand fast in their faith. Soon he was arrested by the Muslims and taken to Delhi. When he refused to become a Muslim he was executed. His son then became the next guru.

The Tenth Guru: Gobind Singh 1666–1708
During the period that Gobind was the guru he made important changes which established the Sikh faith as a permanent separate religion.

In 1708, on the death of Gobind, a most important change took place. Shortly before he died Gobind said that in future the Sikhs would not need a human guru to guide them. Instead they should accept the Granth as their guru. Gobind had edited the book and now it contained all the important Sikh teachings. He declared that the book was the final and immortal guru, and henceforth it should be called 'Guru Granth Sahib' meaning 'Holy Book which is Lord'.

The Sikh Brotherhood
For many years the Sikhs had been under great pressure from their Muslim rulers and Gobind decided, if all else failed, that it was right for Sikhs to defend themselves with the sword. Therefore in 1699 at Anandpur he instituted the Khalsa, the Sikh Brotherhood; members of this would be strong, courageous and ready to give their lives for their faith. The first five members of this brotherhood were chosen by Gobind after they had offered to sacrifice their lives for their guru. They are sometimes known as 'The Beloved Five'. They became members of the Khalsa in a ceremony which Gobind introduced called 'the baptism of the sword'. To show that they were free from the restrictions of the caste system all members of the

Guru Gobind Singh, with the Khalsa which he instituted, from a painting in the Ramarghia Board Sikh Temple, Slough

Khalsa drank a mixture of sugar and water from an iron bowl, and they agreed to share the same surname Singh (meaning 'lion'), which was Gobind's family name. On that day over twenty thousand Sikhs were baptized into the Khalsa.

All members of the Khalsa became 'soldier saints'; they agreed to fight for justice and in defence of their faith. They swore to wear the five Ks all the time (see page 120). The turban became accepted as the symbol of the Brotherhood. In short they became a new army dedicated to a new way of life. Moreover, membership of the Khalsa gave the Sikhs self-respect in a country where everyone was divided into castes according to the strict rules of the Hindu system.

The Khalsa was soon tested by the Muslims. They attacked the Sikhs on many occasions and many Sikhs were killed, but the Khalsa was not broken. Eventually the Mogul Emperor left the Sikhs alone and they lived in peace under the leadership of Gobind Singh.

Later History

For the next one hundred years following the death of Gobind Singh the Muslim Emperors in North India tried to crush the Sikhs altogether. It was a time of great suffering when many Sikhs left their homes and took refuge in the hills. At the end of the 18th century in 1799 a strong Sikh leader, Ranjit Singh, was accepted as ruler of all the Sikhs. He was a great soldier and administrator. By his efforts the Muslims were defeated and the Punjab became an independent state in North-west India. When he died in 1839 the Punjab was strong, but there was no firm ruler to succeed him.

Within a few years war broke out between the Sikhs and the British who were now the rulers in India. By 1850 the Sikhs had been defeated and the Punjab was incorporated into British India. The British respected the Sikh faith, and the Sikhs practised their religion without any interference. However, they felt a need to protect their beliefs and preserve their culture, and eventually they set up their own schools and began to publish their own newspapers.

During the early years of the 20th century the Indian people began to demand freedom from British rule so that they could run their own affairs as they wished. However it was not until 1947, after the Second World War, that they were granted total independence. The Sikhs found that their homeland, the Punjab, was now divided between India and the newly-established country of Pakistan. There was much bitterness which led to open war between Sikhs, Muslims, and Hindus. Eventually the Sikhs settled in Punjab Province which is part of North-west India; in 1966 the Indian Government recognized the area as a Sikh province. Punjabi is its official language and the provincial assembly has a permanent Sikh majority.

The tomb of Ranjit Singh

3 Initiation and Other Ceremonies

The Initiation Ceremony

When Sikh boys and girls are old enough to understand their faith they are initiated into the Sikh community. The ceremony is the same as that which Gobind Singh used when he initiated the first five Sikhs into the Khalsa in 1699 at Anandpur (see page 118).

Preparation

Anyone who accepts Sikh teaching and rules can be baptized into the Sikh community. Any Sikhs (men or women) can conduct the ceremony provided they have kept their baptismal vows. The ceremony can be carried out in any quiet place as long as a copy of the Sikh holy book, the Granth, and five members of the Khalsa are present, with the addition of another who reads from the Granth. The five represent the panj pyares, the original members of the Khalsa when it was instituted by Gobind Singh (see page 118). Before the proceedings begin everyone must have washed thoroughly (including their hair), and the men must be wearing the five Ks (see below). No jewellery can be worn.

The Ceremony

This is called Khanda-di-Pahul, which means 'baptism of the sword'. As a result of being baptized the young people are accepted into the Khalsa. During the ceremony the males also take the vows to keep the five Ks, i.e. kakars. These are very important for Sikhs since they are symbols of their faith and, along with the turban, are worn by all males after baptism.

1 The first of the five Ks is kesh. This means that the men do not cut the hair on their heads or on their faces. It demonstrates their devotion to God by living in harmony with his will.

2 The second K is a comb called the kanga which is used to keep the hair tidy and in place under the turban, and it symbolizes discipline.

3 Sikhs must also wear the kachs, i.e. shorts, usually under their ordinary clothes. These replaced the long loose garment of the Hindus, the dhoti; wearing kachs symbolizes spiritual freedom as Sikhs gave up traditional Hindu ideas.

4 The fourth K is kara which is the wearing of a steel bracelet on the right wrist. It is a symbol of strength, and of the unity of Sikhs in one brotherhood. It also reminds them of their allegiance to the Khalsa and to their religion.

5 The last K is to carry a kirpan, a sword which symbolizes authority and justice, and reminds Sikhs that they must defend their faith by force if necessary, and that God is the defender of Truth. Nowadays, in many countries, it is not normally permitted to carry a sword in public, so Sikhs replace it with a small blade which is often embedded in the kanga.

The Stages of the Ceremony

At the beginning of the Ceremony a Sikh explains the rules of the community; these are to love God, to read and study the Sikh scriptures, to help and serve mankind. The same Sikh then prays, and reads aloud passages from the Granth, while the amrit (baptism nectar) is made in a large iron bowl from water sweetened with sugar and stirred in turn by the Sikhs with a double-edged sword called a Khanda.

The senior Sikh then reads aloud the Japji, the famous poem by Guru Nanak (see pages 116 and 128). The other Sikhs squat in the Vir Asan position (warrior's position), i.e. with the left knee on the floor, but with the right knee raised ready to spring up if an enemy appears. Another poem called the Jap Sahib follows, read by another Sikh, the next in seniority. Then each Sikh reads in turn while the amrit is stirred; this section ends with the reading of an evening prayer called the Anand.

The baptism then takes place. Those to be baptized squat in the Vir Asan position and are given the nectar to drink. Then nectar is sprinkled on to their eyes and hair, and on to their hands five times. They must try not to blink when it goes on their eyes. As this is done, the panj pyares say 'Wahe Guru ji ka Khalsa' (The Khalsa is the chosen of God) and those being baptized reply 'Wahe Guru ji ki fateh' (Victory to God). Any nectar that remains must be drunk. When all the candidates have been baptized the Anand is sung, prayers are said, and lastly all present share in the Kara Prashad, i.e. eating together a food consisting of equal parts of flour, water, sugar and melted butter. After the ceremony males take the additional name Singh just like the first five members of the Khalsa when Gobind Singh initiated them in 1699. Girls take the name 'Kaur' which means 'princess'.

Besides baptism there are other ceremonies held at important times during a Sikh's lifetime, i.e. following the birth of a baby, when Sikhs marry, and at the end of their lives.

Birth

As soon as the mother and the baby are well enough following the birth, they go to the gurdwara with their family, where the first ceremony in the life of a Sikh is carried out. The parents bring the ingredients used in making the Kara Prashad as well as other food to be given out later in the langar. They may also present a romala to the gurdwara; this is a large embroidered cloth used to cover the Granth when it is not being read.

The ceremony begins with the making of the amrit in a bowl while the Japji is recited. The Ardas prayer is offered. It concludes with the prayer that the child may live long and bring joy to its parents. Prayers of thanksgiving are said and the child is dedicated to the service of God. A drop of the amrit is put on the baby's lips and the remainder is drunk by the mother. The Granth is opened at random and the first verse on the page is read out. Then the baby's name is chosen. It must begin with the first letter of the first word of the verse that has been read aloud. The name is announced to the con-

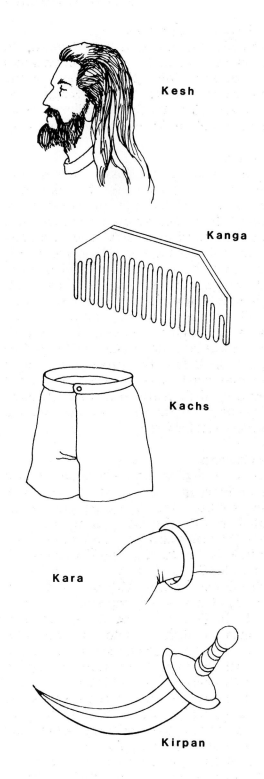

Kesh

Kanga

Kachs

Kara

Kirpan

The Five Ks

A Sikh bride and groom, linked by their scarves, walk round the Granth

gregation and finally the Kara Prashad, which has been made during the ceremony, is shared out amongst all those present.

Marriage

For Sikhs marriage is an important occasion since they believe the souls of the bride and the bridegroom are united into one, and they think that being married is an essential part of life. Marriages are mostly arranged by the parents, although nowadays children have some say in choosing a life partner. No parents would force their children to marry someone they did not want.

The Engagement

When this is announced the girl's parents visit the young man's parents bringing gifts of fruit and coconuts for good luck. Everyone says together the Ardas prayers, which are used regularly in gurdwara worship. The young man is given presents to mark the occasion—a short sword (for ceremonial purposes), a steel bracelet, and perhaps a turban which is a popular gift.

The Wedding Ceremony

The family of the bride makes all the arrangements. On the wedding day the groom and his family, together with friends and guests, go to the gurdwara. However the groom's mother and sisters usually do not attend the ceremony. The groom and his male relatives have refreshments in the langar at the gurdwara before joining the wedding service.

Once in the main hall the groom sits on the floor in front of the Granth. Everyone sings hymns of praise. Then the bride's father puts garlands of flowers round the groom's neck and on the Granth. The bride comes and sits by the groom. She wears the traditional red costume, and has a long scarf over her head and shoulders. Her father places a garland of flowers round her neck as well. The granthi, who takes the marriage service, first says the Ardas prayer while everyone stands. He then gives an address on the duties of married life. Following this, the bride and groom bow to the Granth showing that they accept their duties towards each other.

The bride's father ties her scarf to the groom's scarf or puts the end of the groom's scarf into the bride's hand as a sign that they are man and wife. The special wedding hymn, the Lavan, is now sung and during the singing the bride and groom, linked by their scarves, walk round the Granth four times. Further hymns are sung, including the Anand, the Song of Bliss. After this the bride's mother gives sweets to both the bride and the groom as a sign of welcome to her new son and the grandmother gives the groom a coconut for good luck. The proceedings come to an end with everyone sharing in the eating of Kara Prashad.

A Funeral

As Sikhs believe that death is not the end of a person's existence, but rather a door through which the believer must pass in order to enjoy complete happiness with God, they say that the death of a believer should not be a time of sadness.

According to their traditional practices all Sikhs must be cremated when they die. In the Punjab the dead are cremated on a funeral pyre, but in the West a crematorium is used instead. The body is washed and, if it's a male, dressed with the Five Ks, and wrapped in a shroud before the funeral service is held. Prayers are said; in particular the Sohilla (a bedtime prayer with which Sikhs end each day) is recited as the body is commended to God. Then the cremation begins. Afterwards the ashes of the dead may be scattered on water or buried.

After the funeral, prayers for the dead are said at home or in the gurdwara for the next ten days. Close relatives read the prayers, and sometimes the whole of the Granth is read aloud in a continuous non-stop reading which takes forty-eight hours.

4 The Sikh Place of Worship

The Sikh place of worship is called the gurdwara, which literally means 'the guru's door' or 'the house of the guru'. In the early days of Sikhism a gurdwara was a place where the handwritten copies of the Granth were used in worship, so strictly speaking a gurdwara is a place where a copy of the Granth is kept. Many Sikh homes may have a gurdwara as Sikhs who have room keep a Granth upstairs in a separate place where it is read every day. However the main place for daily corporate worship is a separate building called the gurdwara.

The Outside of the Gurdwara

On the outside the gurdwaras are usually very plain: they do not stand out as buildings of particular importance. The Sikh flag usually flies outside the gurdwara. Its design consists of a double-edge sword, two scimitar-like swords and a circle on a saffron background. This is like the symbol at the beginning of the chapter. Also on the outside the 'ik oanker' symbol (meaning 'God is one Being') may be written or painted. Apart from these there are no distinguishing features.

The Inside of the Gurdwara

The main room in the building is the hall which contains a copy of the Granth; this is where worship takes place. The main feature in the hall is the platform (called 'takht') at the front on which the holy book is placed. This platform or dais is regarded as a throne and it is covered with a silk cloth. A silk cloth also covers the book when it is not being used in worship. Above the book is a silk canopy called the 'palki'. The throne and all the fine silk coverings symbolize authority and sovereignty since the Granth is thought of as a holy book (see page 118).

There is always space around the dais so that worshippers can easily walk round the Granth, for example, at a marriage ceremony. In front of the Granth a cloth is spread out on the floor. This is where gifts of money, fruit, food, etc. are placed. To the side of the dais a place is reserved for the musicians (ragis) who play during worship. The instruments used are small drum, harmonium (small hand-organ) and sitar (a stringed instrument).

Since all the worshippers sit on the floor of the gurdwara, it is usually carpeted for comfort. Around the walls there are pictures of the ten gurus. Apart from the colourful silk cloth on the dais there is little elaborate decoration. At the entrance to the main hall there is a lobby where the worshippers leave their shoes as they may not be worn in the presence of the Granth.

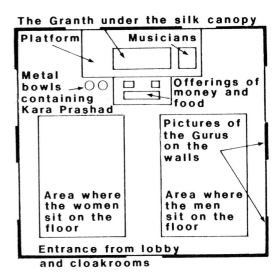

Inside the Golden Temple, showing the musicians and the dais

A plan of a gurdwara

The Langar

The langar (meaning 'free kitchen') or community kitchen has a very important function in the gurdwara. After worship has ended, all those present go into the langar to eat a meal together. This meal is offered freely to Sikhs and non-Sikhs alike, symbolizing the equality of all men before God.

The idea of the langar was introduced very early in Sikhism to show that the Sikhs did not accept all the rules and regulations of the Hindu caste system. All Sikhs must serve in the langar and all visitors, whether rich or poor, important or lowly, sit together and eat the same food.

A building in Bradford which has been converted to a gurdwara

Volunteers prepare bread for the langar in the Golden Temple

The Role of the Gurdwara

The main function of the gurdwara is to provide Sikhs with a place where they can worship God and read the Granth. However, it also acts as the focal point for the local Sikh community. Sikh children meet there in youth clubs, and adults attend weekly meetings to worship as well as to meet informally their friends and relations. In the West the gurdwara has a most important role in providing facilities for teaching Sikh children the principles of their faith. Classes are held regularly where children learn Punjabi so that they can read the Granth properly, and take a full part in worship, as well as learning the doctrines of their faith and how to take their place as adults in Sikh society.

5 Worship

The Sikhs have no special holy day set aside for worship; usually there is an act of worship every evening in the gurdwara. However those Sikhs living in the Western world have adopted Sunday as the regular day in the week for worship. Worship in the gurdwara is led by the granthi. He is a member of the community chosen for this position because he is respected for his wisdom and learning. He is responsible for the care of the gurdwara and the Granth.

Worship in the Gurdwara

Whenever they worship in the gurdwara Sikhs must wear no shoes and have their heads covered. When entering for worship they first approach the Granth, bow and kneel down, placing the forehead on the floor as a sign of respect. They make offerings of food or money which are placed on a cloth spread in front of the Granth. They then take their place sitting on the floor facing the Granth, the men on the right and the women on the left.

Worship is rather informal and can last four or five hours. It consists of readings from the Granth, prayers and hymn singing (called kirtan) which is accompanied by the musicians. Whenever passages from the Granth are read aloud an attendant waves a 'chauri' over the book. A chauri is a kind of fan made from animal hair or peacock's feathers. This action is a symbol of authority or kingship as the Granth is regarded as a royal book. Chauris used to be waved over the heads of kings and rulers in India. Often a senior Sikh talks to the congregation about important subjects connected with their faith.

Worship ends with the saying of a set prayer called the Ardas. For this everyone stands, and one of the Sikhs goes to the front of the congregation and stands facing the Granth. He then prays to God on behalf of all the congregation. First of all a Sikh is asked to remember God and the ten gurus, and to pass on the teachings of the Granth. Next God is asked to bless the Sikh community and all mankind. Then specific prayers are added, e.g. for the sick, the bereaved, the newly-married. During the prayers the Kara Prashad is stirred with a kirpan. This is in a large iron bowl placed near the Granth.

Worship finally closes with the distribution of Kara Prashad. Everyone is given a small portion which they eat with the right hand. By eating together Sikhs show that they are all equal before God. This sharing of food symbolizes the idea that God's nature is to bless mankind, and ensures that no one leaves God's presence hungry.

Daily Devotions

Sikhs are taught to think of themselves as members of the local Sikh community (sangat) as well as the world-wide Sikh brotherhood (panth) and therefore they often worship together. Also since great emphasis is placed on the idea that God is within each human being and on the search for God within oneself, the practice of meditation is an important part of daily devotion.

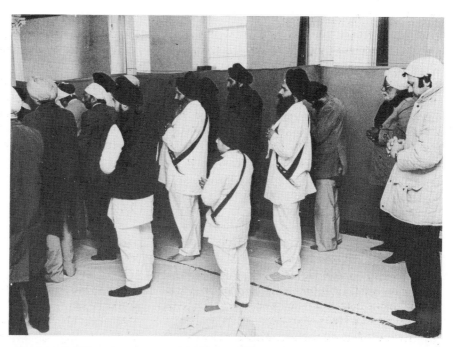

Worshippers in the gurd-wara, showing the karas and kirpans

Nanak taught his followers to pray and meditate twice each day. Every day a Sikh should rise before dawn and wash by having a bath; this symbolizes the washing of the soul in God. Nanak said his followers should begin their devotions by remembering God; he declared 'In the sweet hour of morning meditate on the grace of the True Name'. At sunrise, therefore, Sikhs repeat the Japji and the Jap, which was written by Gobind Singh. Then they think about their founder, Nanak, and the teaching in the scriptures. They also may repeat a famous poem called the Asa-di-var; this was also written by Nanak in praise of God and the Name, and it describes how a man can become a perfect servant of God. This concludes the devotions, but some Sikhs go to the gurdwara to join others in morning worship.

The evening prayers are an important part of daily devotions. Sikhs should say and meditate on two hymns: the Rahiras at dusk and then, just before going to bed, the evening hymn called the Sohilla. They may use a mala—a loop of cotton thread along which 108 knots are tied. This is passed through the fingers as the words 'Wahe Guru' (Wonderful Lord) are repeated many times. If a household has a copy of the Granth, prayers will be held sitting around it. This is done especially in the evening when all the family takes part. First they listen to passages being read aloud and then they spend a short time praying together.

Daily worship is also conducted in the gurdwara. It includes repeating the Asadi-var along with various other hymns, e.g. the Rahiras and the Sukhmani. These hymns express the idea of joining man's soul with God through humility and by serving others.

6 Sikh Beliefs and Teaching

All the main beliefs and teaching of the Sikhs are found in the Granth, the basis of which is the teaching of Nanak himself. The main emphasis of Nanak's writing is the adoration of God.

The 'ik oanker' symbol, which means 'God is one Being'

Nanak first and foremost taught that there is only one God who is worshipped by all the main faiths in the world. Nanak did not name God, but rather referred to Him as 'The Truth' or 'The True Name'. This teaching is summed up in the Mool Mantra, part of the Japji, which begins:

'There is One God
He is the Supreme Truth'.

All Sikhs learn this verse by heart and use it regularly in daily devotions. It is the nearest thing to a creed found in Sikh holy writings. The poem explains that God is Eternal, Supreme Truth, Spirit and Intelligence; that He is Creator, Light, Love and Grace, and that God is Father to the Sikh and every man is his brother.

Nanak taught that man is the Supreme Creation of God; since God is the Creator of all things, He decreed that animals, being lower in creation, should serve mankind. This being so, Sikhs say it is quite permissible for them to eat meat, which was contrary to Hindu teaching.

Nanak also believed that although the world is real and good, men never see it as it really is; they only see a false picture. When men find God in themselves and in all things in the world they will experience peace of mind; as a result they will live truly as God wills and they will be free from suffering.

The Hindu ideas of reincarnation and the law of karma are part of Sikh belief. This means that, as all men are part of the cycle of birth, death and rebirth, a man's soul will be reborn in another body according to the way he has lived in his previous life. Nanak said a man's aim should be to reach Nirvana, i.e. to know the full forgiveness of God and to experience eternal fellowship with him, and the way to accomplish this is to seek to live with God. Nanak taught that a Sikh will be on the right path to reach Nirvana if he keeps the vows he made at baptism. In practice this means meditating on God regularly, actively living a good life, serving others, living in peace and being tolerant of the ways and beliefs of other people. However

Nanak explained that living a life of sin condemns a man to another life on earth, but with the hope that Nirvana can be reached by living a much better life than before.

From the very beginning Nanak rejected the caste system which was so deeply rooted in Indian life. He believed that, as God was in all people, all are equal, and so it was wrong to divide people into castes. Everyone should be treated equally regardless of race or religion, whether rich or poor, men or women. This was put into practice by introducing the langar into the gurdwara (see page 124). Furthermore, since men and women are treated equally, Sikhs have no priests, and any Sikh, male or female, can lead worship.

These beliefs affect their ordinary everyday living. In order to serve God to the best of their ability Sikhs are instructed to work hard 'with hands, head and heart', and not to live on the charity of others. Sikhs are taught to be unselfish and to expect no rewards in this life or the next; so they give donations of money and food to their faith, and help in every practical way possible. Also since they believe life is a gift from God, they say it is wrong to abuse their bodies in any way, and so the drinking of alcohol and smoking of tobacco should be avoided.

7 Sikh Holy Writings

Most of the Sikh sacred writings are found in two books. The first is the Adi Granth (the name means 'first collection' or 'first book'). It contains the writings of many of the ten gurus and of important Muslim and Hindu teachers. It was compiled over a period of 200 years, mainly by Guru Angad, Guru Arjun Dev and Guru Gobind Singh, who edited the final version.

The Dasam Granth (meaning 'collection of the tenth guru') is the second book and it contains the writings of Gobind Singh. His writing is only found in this second volume as he did not wish to include any of his own work when the final edition of the Adi Granth was produced.

The Compilation of the Adi Granth

The first version was produced when Angad was the second guru. It included many poems of Nanak and Kabir as well as some of Angad's own writing. Angad also devised a written form of Punjabi called 'gurmukhi', which was used when the contents of the Granth were written down.

Arjun Dev was the main compiler of the book. To the collected writings of the earlier gurus he added the writings of Hindu and Muslim wise men, e.g. Kabir and Jaidev, whose teaching was similar to that of the gurus, and some of his own writing. All this was written down in Punjabi, the Sikhs' language. But for Arjun much of the writing of Indian holy men would have been lost, since the Granth contains some of the finest religious literature ever written. Arjun's edition of the Granth has been carefully preserved and today it is on display in a glass case in a building called the Harimandir in Amritsar.

The final version of the Granth was made by Gobind Singh, the tenth guru. It now contains the writings of six gurus, of other Sikh writers, e.g. Satta and Murdana, and of twelve non-Sikhs including Kabir, Jaidev, Sheikh Farid, Namdev and Ravides. In 1708 Gobind changed the status of the Granth by pronouncing it the final and everlasting guru, and from that time it has been called Guru Granth Sahib (see page 118).

The Contents of the Granth

The entire content of the Granth is made up of hymns called shabads, and poems praising God or exhorting men to listen to His voice. The book begins with a verse written by Nanak called the Mool Mantra (see page 128); this name means 'perfect mantra'. A mantra is a sacred chant often passed on by a Guru to his disciples, and it contains the key to divine knowledge and to communication with God; it can give the name of God and explain how God should be addressed. After the Mool Mantra comes the remainder of the Japji, which is the most important of the Sikh hymns and its main theme is the nature of God.

Then follow 200 odes and hymns written by Nanak, the most important of which is the Asa-di-var. A group of hymns called Rahiras come next; the most popular of these is the Sukhmani written by Arjun Dev. The final group of writings is a collection of poems of great beauty by Kabir and other non-Sikh writers.

The Arrangement of the Granth

Arjun Dev introduced a definite order when compiling the Granth. He arranged the col-lection of the hymns into thirty-one sections. Each section has a different musical tune, or 'raga', with the exception of the Japji and a few verses at the end of the book which are spoken.

In each section the hymns of the gurus are in a special order beginning with those of Nanak. The hymns and poems of the non-Sikh writers follow with those of Kabir first. Each section also has a particular Indian musical form, e.g. Ramkali, which is used whenever the hymns are sung.

At first copies of the Granth were hand-written; it was not printed until the 19th century. However each copy produced is an exact replica of the edition produced by Gobind Singh. Thus every copy of the Granth

A Sikh reads from the Granth while an attendant waves the chauri

has 5894 hymns written on 1430 pages. Each hymn is always found on the same page, e.g. page 917, the Sohilla, the evening hymn of Nanak; page 773, the Lavan, the wedding hymn by Ram Das.

The Status of the Granth

As we have already mentioned, before he died Gobind Singh declared that the Granth would be his successor. From that time on it was regarded as the final and immortal guru. In future he said it was not necessary to have further human gurus; everything that a Sikh needed to know about his faith was written in the Granth, and they should turn to it for the God-inspired words of the guru.

As the Granth is the guru of the Sikhs they regard it with special reverence and respect. This is shown in several ways. The book has a place of honour in the gurdwara, being placed on a throne, and all Sikhs sit on the floor in the gurdwara below the level of the book. Whenever passages are chanted or read in the gurdwara, the chauri is waved over the book. Also during worship in the gurdwara, Sikhs never turn their backs on the book. Moreover, whenever they enter a room containing the Granth, Sikhs have their heads covered, wear no shoes on their feet, and they bow in front of the book, just as they would when paying respect to a human guru 300 years before.

8 Pilgrimage

The Sikh gurus did not encourage their followers to visit holy places on pilgrimage. They felt that it was more important for a man to have a change of heart by which he improves his whole attitude and approach to life. For this reason they say man should meditate on the presence of God within himself.

However Amritsar, being the centre of the Sikh faith, has become a place that Sikhs like to visit. Most of all they like to visit the Golden Temple which is situated in the city.

The Golden Temple at Amritsar

You will remember that the fourth guru, Ram Das, ordered the pool and the island to be constructed, but the temple itself was built during the time of Arjun Dev, the fifth guru.

The temple is a low building (with steps down to it) symbolizing humility before God. It has a door on each of its four sides to show that it is open to all men, in particular to the four major castes, no matter of what faith, class or race. Causeways run across the pool to the island so that people can easily visit the temple. It is called the Golden Temple because its dome and upper storey are covered with gold leaf.

Sikhs who visit the temple like to take a bath in the pool or tank, and then walk past the Guru Granth Sahib which 'sits on its throne' in the Temple. They will listen to the readings which go on continuously throughout the day. They can arrange to have passages read on their behalf to remind them of times of happiness or of sorrow. They also may be present to see the special rituals which are observed in the morning and at night. Each morning the Granth is carried ceremoniously into the temple in a chest, and then returned in the evening to the building where it is kept. To carry the Granth in the procession is considered a great honour.

9 Festivals

Sikhism, like other religions, has festival days which have an important religious significance. These days are of two types: melas, which are meetings or fairs, and gurpurbs, which are holidays associated with the gurus.

Melas
These correspond to Hindu festivals, but their meaning has been changed by the Sikhs. The three celebrated are Baisakhi, Diwali and Hola Mohalla.

Baisakhi
This is the only fixed festival in the Sikh calendar. It falls on 13th April and is the beginning of the Sikh New Year. In India it marks the beginning of harvest and the hot dry summer. It is an occasion in the year when all Sikhs should assemble. However, above all, it is remembered as the birthday of Sikhism for it was on this day in 1699 that Gobind Singh instituted the Khalsa at Anandpur. So it is the day for admitting new members to the Sikh community by the baptism ceremony. All the women wear new clothes and the men exchange turbans. In Amritsar a great fair is held when farmers sell many animals, mainly horses, camels and pigs. In the Punjab farmers by tradition do not begin to harvest the first corn crop until Baisakhi has ended.

Baisakhi is also the anniversary of a number of battles the Sikhs fought against the Mogul Emperors in the early years of their faith, and of the massacre at Jallianwala Bagh in Amritsar in 1919 when over 2000 people were killed or injured by British troops. The Sikhs had refused to cancel the traditional Baisakhi fair, and would not disperse when ordered.

Diwali
This occurs in the late autumn. For Hindus it is the annual festival of lights when the victory of good over evil is celebrated; however Sikhs commemorate the release of the sixth guru, Har Gobind. He had been imprisoned by the Mogul Emperor, and on his return to Amritsar the Golden Temple was lit up with many lamps. Nowadays Sikhs celebrate Diwali as a festival of freedom with bonfires and fireworks. In Sikh homes lamps are lit and presents exchanged. In Amritsar the Golden Temple is illuminated.

Hola Mohalla
This was introduced in 1680 by Gobind Singh to replace the Hindu festival of Holi. Today it is only seriously celebrated in An-

andpur in the Punjab. It occurs in March, and in Gobind's time it was a day for organizing mainly military events, for instance mock battles and competitions in horsemanship. Nowadays a three-day fair is held with horse-riding events and athletic competitions; generally it is an occasion for much light-hearted fun.

Gurpurbs

These are holidays when events associated with particular gurus are remembered. Although these gurpurbs remember different events they are all celebrated in a similar way. On these days in India open-air processions are held when the Guru Granth Sahib is taken round the streets escorted by five Sikh men carrying swords. The crowd carries banners, and the women, especially, sing hymns. Occasionally the procession stops, then speakers address the crowds and poetry is read aloud.

The gurpurb is always held on the weekend following the anniversary day of the particular event being celebrated. This is to allow as many people as possible to attend. All the speeches, sermons, hymn singing, etc. concern the guru whose life and work are remembered on that occasion. Outside India the celebrations are only held in the gurdwara.

The most important event is a complete continuous reading of the Granth. This begins about forty-eight hours before the Sunday worship and is carried out by a succession of readers. Sikhs try to attend for some of the time, however short, each day. All are present when the final pages are read. Worship then follows, and it concentrates on the guru who is being remembered. When worship is over everyone goes into the langar for a meal.

There are four important gurpurbs held during the year. In January it is the birthday of Gobind Singh, and in November of Nanak, the first guru and founder of Sikhism. The two other gurpurbs remember, on the other hand, solemn events; for instance in June the martyrdom of Arjun Dev, who was tortured to death by the Muslims at Lahore, and in December the martyrdom of Teg Bahadur who was executed on the orders of the Mogul Emperor in 1675.

·Glossary·

Amrit	mixture of water and sugar used in baptism (cf. page 120)
Amritsar	the holy city of the Sikhs in the Punjab and centre of the Sikh faith (cf. page 131)
Anand	an evening prayer (cf. page 120)
Ardas	set prayer used at the end of public worship (cf. page 126)
Asa-di-var	important poem written by Nanak in praise of God (cf. page 127)
Baisakhi	festival held in April; the beginning of the Sikh New Year (cf. page 132)
Chauri	kind of fan waved over the Granth when it is read aloud (cf. page 126)
Dhoti	loose garment worn by Hindu men (cf. page 120)
Diwali	festival held in late autumn celebrating the release of the sixth guru from prison (cf. page 132)
Five Ks	the five kakars or symbols of the Sikh faith; connected with five vows taken at baptism (cf. page 120)
Golden Temple	the Sikh's most famous gurdwara, situated in Amritsar (cf. page 131)
Gobind Singh	the tenth guru of the Sikhs (cf. page 118)
Granth	Sikh holy book; the full name is Guru Granth Sahib (cf. page 129)
Granthi	official who cares for the gurdwara and officiates at some ceremonies (cf. page 126)
Gurdwara	Sikh place of worship which means 'the house of the guru' (cf. page 123)
Gurmukhi	written form of Punjabi, the Sikh language (cf. page 116)
Gurpurb	festivals or holidays associated with the gurus (cf. page 133)
Guru	religious teacher; one of the ten Sikh religious leaders (cf. page 115)
Guru Granth Sahib	see **Granth**
Harimandir	a gurdwara in Amritsar in which an early edition of the Granth is preserved (cf. page 129)
Hola Mohalla	festival held in March; replaces Hindu festival of Holi (cf. page 132)
Ik Oanker	means 'God is one Being'; a Sikh symbol represented by two Punjabi letters (cf. page 123)
Jap	poem written by Gobind Singh (cf. page 127)
Japji	poem written by Nanak which is the basis of his teaching about God (cf. page 116)
Kabir	Hindu teacher who greatly influenced Nanak's religious ideas (cf. page 115)
Kachs	one of the Five Ks; shorts worn by all Sikh men (cf. page 120)
Kakars	see **Five Ks**
Kanga	one of the Five Ks; a comb worn under the turban to keep the hair tidy and in place (cf. page 120)
Kara	one of the Five Ks; a steel bracelet (cf. page 120)
Kara Prashad	food eaten after worship; a mixture of butter, flour, sugar and water (cf. page 121)
Karma	see Hindu glossary

Kaur	additional name given to Sikh girls at baptism; means 'princess' (cf. page 121)
Kesh	one of the Five Ks; a rule not to cut any of the hair on the head or face (cf. page 120)
Khalsa	the Sikh brotherhood, which Sikhs join on being baptized (cf. page 118)
Khanda	doube-edged sword used in religious ceremonies (cf. page 120)
Khanda-di-Pahul	name of the Sikh baptism ceremony (cf. page 120)
Kirpan	one of the Five Ks; a sword (cf. page 120)
Kirtan	Sikh hymn singing (cf. page 126)
Langar	communal kitchen or dining hall in a gurdwara (cf. page 124)
Lavan	special wedding hymn (cf. page 123)
Mala	loop of cotton thread (like a rosary), used in private prayer (cf. page 128)
Mela	type of Sikh festival (cf. page 132)
Mool Mantra	beginning of the Japji; sums up Nanak's teaching about God (cf. page 128)
Nanak	the first of the ten gurus; founder of the Sikh faith (cf. page 115)
Nirvana	see Buddhist glossary
Palki	the silk canopy erected over the takht in the gurdwara (cf. page 123)
Panj Pyares	the original five members of the Khalsa (cf. page 120)
Panth	the worldwide brotherhood of Sikhs (cf. page 126)
Punjab	region of North-west India, homeland of the Sikhs (cf. page 115)
Punjabi	the Sikh language (cf. page 116)
Ragis	Sikh musicians who accompany hymn singing (cf. page 124)
Rahiras	Sikh hymns used regularly in worship (cf. page 128)
Romala	embroidered cloth which covers the Granth when it is not being used (cf. page 121)
Sangat	the local Sikh community (cf. page 126)
Shabads	hymns used in worship (cf. page 129)
Sikh	means 'one who learns'; a follower of the Sikh religion (cf. page 116)
Singh	means 'lion'; additional name given to all Sikh men at baptism (cf. page 119)
Sitar	type of stringed musical instrument used in worship (cf. page 124)
Sohilla	an evening prayer composed by Nanak; used regularly in daily devotions (cf. page 128)
Sukhmani	hymn used frequently in worship (cf. page 128)
Takht	platform in the gurdwara on which the Granth is placed (cf. page 123)
Vir Asan	warrior's position adopted in some religious ceremonies (cf. page 120)
Wahe Guru	sacred saying used in worship; means 'Wonderful Lord' (cf. page 128)

·Activities·

1 Important Things to Remember and Understand

Special Sikh words, e.g. Sikh; guru; gurdwara; Granth; the Five Ks; Kara Prashad; amrit; granthi.

2 Important Things to Find out

Find out about your nearest Sikh community and visit the gurdwara, remembering to respect their rules. Try their food in the langar.
Invite a Sikh to visit your school to talk about his or her faith.

3 Important Things to Discuss

What do you think are the most important things for Sikhs in their religion?
What difficulties do Sikhs living in this country have to face?
What should Sikhs do if the laws of a country contradict their religious rules?

4 Important Things to Do

Design some posters illustrating important aspects of Sikhism, e.g. the Five Ks with a Sikh wearing a turban.
Try preparing Sikh food.

5 Written Work

a Write a description of a Sikh baptism as if it were your own, explaining your feelings.
b Describe a visit to a gurdwara; explain what you would see and what takes place when the Sikhs worship.
c Write about the Sikh holy book explaining why it is so important in their religion.